Street Tales

Tales

Volume One

by Tyler Martin

Edited by Lil Barcaski

Published by: GWN Publishing
www.GWNPublishing.com

Cover Design: Kristina Conatser

ISBN: 978-1-965971-20-8

DEDICATION

I started my law enforcement career in 2011 and it changed the trajectory of my life and the lives of my family. I started the Street Tales podcast to memorialize the stories throughout my career for my children. I spent so much time away from them as they grew up and sitting here in my 40's, I don't know if it was worth it. The best I can do is to try and capture the stories of the men and women who have impacted my life and by extension their lives.

How do you define the world of law enforcement, the good, the bad, the heartbreaking, and the miraculous stories that are created each and every day? How can you describe what makes a successful law enforcement professional, the importance of the men and women who have taken on the mantel to serve their communities and their country? Short answer, I have no idea. I attempt to capture and answer these questions through individual's stories and experiences on the Street Tales podcast and now this book!

First, my family, who have stood by me and put up with my highs and lows as I pursued this career in law enforcement. They have always stood by me in my triumphs and my darkest hours and never made me feel like I was doing this alone. Second, my friends, who have walked a similar path as me, and have also gone to the dark places. The ability to share my dreams and nightmares with them and know they understand is priceless to me.

To the first responders, veterans, and those touched by the law enforcement community your work and dedication do not go unnoticed. You are not alone and your work and dedication matter to the men and women you protect and serve.

TABLE OF CONTENTS

FOREWORD

Tyler Martin's *Street Tales* is precisely the kind of raw, honest narrative our veteran and first responder communities, and frankly, the wider world, desperately needs. As someone who has personally navigated the shadows of service and confronted the truth about trauma, I recognize the profound courage it takes to share these stories, and Tyler and his guests do so with remarkable vulnerability.

This powerful collection humanizes the law enforcement profession, moving beyond the uniform to expose the heartache and tragedy on an indiscernible level that officers and their families endure.

Street Tales bravely tackles the profound and often unspoken realities of life in service, mirroring my own experiences with the gritty, visceral, and gut-wrenching impact of traumatic events. It delves into the immense cost of such a career, affecting not just the individual but also their loved ones, who bore the brunt of the trauma and decisions undeservingly.

What truly sets *Street Tales* apart is its unwavering commitment to breaking the stigma of mental health in the law enforcement community. My own journey has taught me the critical importance of finally being honest with myself and my loved ones about my trauma, fears, the monster, or my insecurities hidden in the shadows, and realizing that I was never alone. Tyler's platform, particularly through figures like Monique Greco and Bjar Atkins, champions open dialogue and challenges the deeply ingrained culture of stoicism that often isolates those who serve.

The narratives within *Street Tales* powerfully illustrate the journey from adversity to resilience, emphasizing how individuals can move from victimhood to growth. It showcases inspiring individuals like Monte Duncan, Dave Tarbox, and Joe Caputo, who didn't allow a victim mindset to define the rest of their lives. Their transformations, from navigating addiction, criminal activity, and dark paths to embracing rehabilitation, growth, and success, demonstrate the immense power of owning one's journey and charting a new course. The experiences of Adam Macaluso, from combat to diverse law enforcement roles, further highlight this remarkable capacity for post-traumatic growth.

Street Tales offers invaluable and diverse perspectives, from law enforcement to those who have encountered the system from different angles. This range of voices enriches understanding and fosters the emotional intelligence necessary to navigate complex human interactions. The book, through figures like Monique Greco, also imparts practical wisdom, stressing that the first and foremost fundamental thing you have to know how to do in this job is to communicate. The powerful examples of mentorship and unwavering support among teammates, as seen in Tyler's relationships with Bjar and Mo, resonate deeply with my own belief that no one gets through it alone.

Tyler Martin's *Street Tales* is more than just a collection of stories from conversations; it's an essential tool for healing, understanding, and fostering genuine connection. It reminds us that behind every uniform, and in every life, there is a complex human story struggling to be heard. I wholeheartedly endorse this book and encourage everyone to read it, share its truth, and let it be a catalyst for the vital conversations that truly matter.

- **Doug White, author of *Hiding In Plain Sight***

ENDORSEMENTS

"From the street to the beat, get the straight dope from both sides of the badge. Street Tales provides a rare, unfiltered peek inside the lives of cops and criminals to expose broader themes of hope, redemption, and grit."

- Josh Bates, LtCol USMC (Retired), author of The Baghdad Shuffle

---

"Street Tales showcases stories from both those in the law enforcement profession along with those who have battled addiction and being on the wrong side of the law. This book has a unique way of showing the reader how, as human beings, we are all connected by more than our job titles or the situations we find ourselves in life. These stories are proof that we can all overcome adversity.

"Tyler is an example of perseverance through life pushing back. Seeing adversity as a direction shift to embrace, Tyler wasn't afraid to change course in pursuit of his passion of service to others.

"The stories you read should serve as a subtle reminder that you are not alone in your struggle. Many others have found growth on the

other side of their pain and missteps having traveling a similar path as you. Street Tales is a window into what's possible.

-Jason M. Palamara, author of Living Blue

INTRODUCTION

by Podcast Host Tyler Martin

I grew up as the child of two Marines in the 80's. I was conceived in Japan and born in North Carolina on a Marine Corp base. I was no stranger to moving around growing up and that lifestyle followed me for the rest of my life. My parents were hardcore Marines, and I was indoctrinated into the Marine Corp mindset early on in my childhood. It was rough growing up with divorced parents living on a Marine salary. My earliest memories are of living on military bases or in trailer parks for the majority of my childhood. Nothing was ever easy or given to me, even as a child.

With that being said, one of the greatest regrets of my life was not joining the military, but my life went in a different direction. I was recruited by Tennessee State University, a Historically Black College University (HBCU), to play football. That is where I met one of my lifelong friends, Monte Duncan. We will go through his story later in the book. Before I graduated college, my son was born, and this changed the trajectory of my life. I was a business major and was planning on being a millionaire before I turned 30 years old. Instead, I bounced around as a manager of retail locations, a short stint at Enterprise Rent a Car, and finally settled in as a Financial Specialist with Wachovia Bank. That was during the financial crisis in 2008, and I quickly learned how tumultuous the bank industry is. I was making more money than I had ever made in my life, but it was taken away from me in the blink of an eye. I was not happy professionally and was looking for a job with a team atmosphere.

The Hillsborough County Sheriff's Office (HCSO) was hiring and I threw my name in the hat to become a Deputy Sheriff. I can assure you that none of my friends or family would have ever dreamed that I would get into the law enforcement profession. After several interviews, polygraphs, and a battery of tests, I was hired. But in the law enforcement world, that is step one. After that, you have to go through a police academy, field training, and then depending on the agency, a probationary period.

At the time I was hired, HCSO had a two-week paramilitary boot camp that ended up being one of the hardest times of my life. We were up at 4 a.m. and usually started the day with a two to three mile run every morning and physical training/punishments that lasted all day, scattered in between training and learning how to be a Deputy Sheriff. That was where Bjar Atkins came into my life and eventually become my best friend, confidant, and wartime consigliere when needed. After a few years on as a baby deputy, Bj and I met Monique Greco (Mo). During my time at HCS, her friendship and guidance made me a better Deputy and a better person. Mo got me through some really difficult times professionally and personally. We get into Bjar Atkins and Monique Greco's stories later on in the book as well.

HCSO is where I learned how to be a cop. I had several excellent life-altering supervisors and others who stabbed me in the back as soon as they met me. Needless to say, I learned a lot in a short amount of time about the politics in law enforcement and not all supervisors are equal. During this transitionary period in my life, I was attempting to be a husband, and a father to my son and newly added daughter. It was a lot to juggle, and I did not handle the responsibilities very well. I decided I needed another change and applied to the Federal Bureau of Investigation (FBI).

I was selected by the FBI, and in the process, had to move my family from Florida to Maine while I was in training. I was riding as high as I could at this point and felt that finally my life was on track! I made it a total of nine weeks at the FBI before being told they did not like my push-up form, and they let me go. I wish I was joking but that is literally what crushed my dreams of becoming a Special Agent for the FBI. Needless to say, I did not take it well and was devastated.

I was lucky that after being drummed out of the FBI, the Maine State Police (MSP) gave me shot to become a Maine State Trooper. Once again, I was headed to another academy, this one only nine weeks long. I will say this was some of the best training I ever received in my life as far as law enforcement training is concerned. I became a Maine State Trooper, and I absolutely loved my time with them. Remembering I had a family to support, I was not making enough money to sustain our life, and so, I began looking for a way to level up. I still had the desire to become a Special Agent as I felt that was the next step in my career.

I applied and was hired by the United States Secret Service (USSS), which was exciting and nerve-racking as well. I had the recent failure with the FBI fresh on my mind and felt guilty as I had just started with the Maine State Police, but my family obligation trumped any hesitations I could muster. Once again, I was leaving my family for another academy, this time to Glynco, GA, followed by several months in Beltsville, MD.

My time as a Special Agent with the U.S. Secret Service was amazing, for the most part. I traveled the world and protected some of the most powerful men and women in the world. But I was gone more and more from my children, leaving their care and raising to their mother. During that time frame I met Dave Tarbox, who became a close friend and is someone who has also shared his amazing story with me which will be discussed later in the book.

I spent seven years as a Special Agent with the U.S. Secret Service before finally pulling the plug on that career as well. I was basically in training or traveling for the majority of my children's lives and went several months without seeing them at a time. My son graduated high school and joined the Marines, and I wanted to be there for my daughter's final two years of high school.

I often ask myself if it was all worth it and if I should have chosen a different career path as I missed so much of my children's lives. They loved the stories and the gifts I would bring them from my travels but that doesn't replace the time lost. Once I left the U.S. Secret Service, I met Joe Caputo and Adam Macaluso, two men with very different backgrounds and life trajectories. Adam and Joe have amazing stories of their life experiences and have become close friends in a very short time. Their stories are discussed later in the book as well!

I talked to my children for several years about starting a podcast and writing a book to document and discuss my time in law enforcement. Almost as a way to explain to them why I was gone so much and what I was doing instead of being there for them. I came across an old family VHS tape that had a two-minute snippet of my late grandfather's voice on it. He didn't really say anything deep on the recording, but hearing his voice brought tears to my eyes and that was the turning point for me to start the podcast, Street Tales. I wanted to leave something behind for my children to listen to when I am long gone and try and capture the stories that I have heard or collected thus far in my life. I have met so many interesting people and heard amazing and horrific stories for over a decade.

Street Tales started with a 20-minute solo episode of me just talking into a microphone lol. It has grown to contain stories of some of my closest friends and family to heads of agencies and experts in the various fields that impact law enforcement. This book is a collection of a few of those stories and an introduction to Street Tales team and the podcast. I am hoping to expose the humanity of the law enforcement profession. These are stories of great men and women who dedicated their lives to protecting their communities and the struggles they had to go through. I also want to capture stories of individuals who chose a different path and had many encounters with law enforcement, both good and bad, but who have been able to overcome their past decisions and become successful in their own rights.

The field of Law Enforcement is hard to capture in a few short sentences, and yet it is such an important aspect of our everyday lives. The first three sections of this book are stories of addiction, criminal activity, and dark paths explored followed by rehabilitation, growth, and success. The last three sections of this book go through the process of becoming a law enforcement professional from very different prospectives and paths. Please join me on this journey as I introduce to you the Street Tales team and share some powerful stories of those close to me.

Click or scan the QR Code
to hear the podcast interview

with **Monte Duncan**

The Story of
MONTE DUNCAN

M onte Duncan and I met at Tennessee State University (TSU) in the summer of 2002. We were both scholarship athletes for the TSU Football team. Monte came from Atlanta, GA, and I came from Sarasota, FL. As freshman athletes, we started practice two weeks before the rest of the team and approximately a month before school started. This was back in the day when three-a-day practices were the norm, and we were learning the plays, working out, and adapting to our new lives as college athletes. I can remember after a particularly brutal practice looking over at Monte and telling him, "This is just practice, bro; we don't have to go so hard against each other." Monte laughed and said, "Man, I was going to say the same thing to you".

TSU is a Historically Black College University (HBCU) and as such, played six HBCU Classics a year, and offered minority scholarships to white minorities; this comes up in the conversation with Monte below. I was typically the only white person on the team and in most of my classes. There would be white athletes that came and went but I started my college football life at TSU and wanted to finish at TSU. I later learned that this is not the norm when it comes to college athletes especially in football. TSU had athletes that would come play for a season or two from larger schools or smaller schools to get playing time and then move on to whatever path they felt was better for them. I also learned that most larger football programs offer their athletes two-year scholarships, and you have to earn any additional years. There were 25 athletes my freshman year, and I believe only five or six finished their college time at TSU for various reasons.

During my time at TSU, Monte and I developed a friendship that has lasted over 20 years. Monte would stay with me over the summer sometimes or when he needed somewhere to stay as I lived off campus. During that time, I learned about Monte's life and how he came to be a college athlete at TSU. Monte grew up in Atlanta, GA, and grew up in a violent and difficult area of Atlanta. His dad was not around and addicted to drugs and his mother did her best to raise Monte as a single mom. At a young age Monte found himself on the street, creating a family from other men/children in his same predicament. Monte had to learn and adapt quickly to his surroundings, and luckily, he was always large for his age. This would help him as he would have to defend himself from grown men and teenagers even when he was in elementary school. He lived in an area that had high drug use and sales, and the cops had declared that area a high-crime area and would stop and harass Monte incessantly throughout his adolescent life. They would tackle and detain Monte on a regular basis even though he lived in the area and clearly had a reason to be there. Monte has been shot at, had to hide from rival gangs/drug dealers, and was forced to grow up rapidly in a very dangerous and confusing area.

Through all of this, Monte was able to stay focused, finish school, obtain a college degree, and be a scholar athlete. Monte is a father, invested in his community to this day, and works in the local school district where he grew up. He's a good person and a good man and has learned from the decisions he made in his youth. He's focused on continuing to set an example, not only for his children, but for the next generation.

Below is a conversation between Monte and I:

FROM GRIDIRON TO LIFE'S SIDELINES:
A Journey with Monte Duncan

STREET TALES: *In the summer of 2002, Monte Duncan and I became teammates for the Tennessee State University Tigers located in Nashville, TN. Monte was number 99, and I was number 88. We played college football back in the day when teams would have two to three practices a day, and it was a grind. During that time, Monte and I were going hard as shit against each other and realized we were doing so because the other was going hard as well. At that point we became friends, and it has carried over for over 20 years. We did lose contact for a little bit after college and now we're 40-year-old men.*

MONTE DUNCAN: I'm excited to be on here with you and anything for my brother! I'm from Atlanta, GA, the real Atlanta, GA. I was raised in the bluff, and I stayed in the bluff my whole life.

If you're from any other part of Georgia, you can't say you're from Atlanta. You were the first person I met in college and the first friend I made in college. I must also say, you were my first white friend as well.

In Atlanta, I went to a high school called Washington High School, which is a majority black school. Tyler is my first white friend and the coolest person I ever met in my life.

I do remember that first week of practice, and we both were going hard trying to earn a spot on the team and kind of proving ourselves. I think for the most part it was a mentality that we both shared and being in a new place, new school, playing college ball, it was a lot. I remember my coaches wanted me to go to a military school, but I just couldn't do the military thing. Tennessee State found me and gave me a full ride.

STREET TALES: *What was it like growing up in Atlanta, GA?*

MONTE DUNCAN: Growing up in Atlanta was not easy and I grew up in a poor home. My mom did everything she could for us and to this day I don't know how or where she was able to get some of the things we had in our home. I respect my mom more now that I am grown and have children of my own. I can only imagine how hard it was for her.

I never had a dad in my life because he was always on drugs, and he is still on drugs. My mom was both my mom and my dad. It was a rocky road growing up.

STREET TALES: *Where did you go to high school in Atlanta?*

MONTE DUNCAN: I went to Booker T. Washington High School and that's where I really learned how to play football! Booker T. Washington is one of the best high schools in Atlanta, and there are a bunch of big alumni that graduated from there. Martin Luther King is probably the most notable alumni that I can think of.

STREET TALES: *What was it like growing up in the Bluff?*

MONTE DUNCAN: Heroin is big in the Bluff, and I have seen some of the most amazing shit in my life and some of the scariest shit. I grew up on Griffin Street which was right next to a store where dudes would hangout and slang dope. There would be as many as 50 people hanging out at the store, and I remember when I was young thinking, they were going to play football or something, which was foolish, looking back.

One day, I walked down to the store to see what was going on and immediately they were asking me what I wanted and trying to sell me drugs. I didn't do any drugs, but I was alone, and I gravitated to these dudes. They became my homeboys. Everyone must pick their own path, and I feel like we were all in survival mode back then and you would not survive alone. I started hanging out with my homeboys and selling dope was part of that. We were able to buy our own clothes, shoes, cars, food; I mean anything we wanted. I remember one of my homeboys bought his first car when he was in eighth grade, man. That's how much money was going around in the neighborhood at the time.

STREET TALES: *What was that like for you?*

MONTE DUNCAN: I was in middle school, man, so studying or thinking about my future wasn't really on my mind then. I wanted to make money and keep up with my homeboys. I had to lie to my mother because she wasn't with that shit and would've beat my ass if she knew I was selling dope.

I tried to be sneaky at first, and I remember selling a cut up bar of soap to some crackhead. I cut up the soap into little packages and was slanging it as dope. I made like $300 off a bar of soap. But I was young and stupid and didn't think about the fact that the crackheads would come looking for me for selling them soap. We found out there was this dangerous dude, Jay, looking for us, and he was going to kill us.

Me and my homeboys laid low for a few days, but I was like, *fuck it, man, I can't live this way.*

After maybe three days, I ran into Jay in the store by my house and everyone hanging around the store wanted to see what I was going to do. Jay was a grown man, and I was in eighth grade at the time, but I walked up to him and knocked his ass out. After that day, I got a reputation for fighting and folks feared me, thinking I always wanted to fight. The truth is I don't like to fight, and I never really wanted to fight with anyone. At the same time, I didn't want to be scared, and if you don't fight in that neighborhood, then your life is going to be difficult.

STREET TALES: *When did you start playing football?*

MONTE DUNCAN: I started playing football my freshman year of high school. I had a reputation for fighting and even got kicked out of middle school for a little while and like I mentioned before, my mom wasn't on that shit.

I had already grown up with the mindset to defend my homeboys, and I was known for my one hitter quitter; I could knock dudes out with one hit and that scared a lot of people. The idea of defending my teammates came naturally to me and still does to this day. At my high school, if you weren't on the football team, then nobody cared about what you were doing, and the football players got all the attention and the girls, so I wanted that for myself as well.

Historical Violence and Drug Abuse

STREET TALES: *You mentioned the area you grew up in was dangerous, and the cops were very aggressive even if you lived there. Can you elaborate on that?*

MONTE DUNCAN: There was a lot of gang shit in my neighborhood, and I can remember a day when my homeboys got into a fight with the Blue Jean Bandits or something like that. I knocked a couple them dudes out, and they pulled out yacht sticks (guns) and before that time I had never seen guns like that in my life. Me and my homeboys had to run for our life because they were shooting at our asses. I don't know why I fought so much other than I was in survival mode, and I thought it was fun at the time. I am too old for that shit now man, lol!

The bluff is called zone one, and there was a law enforcement group called Red Dog. Red Dog was the most ruthless fucking gang unit in the fucking world. I don't give a damn what city you're from or where you have been, Red Dog is known everywhere. [1]

I was walking home one day from high school, and this officer we called Goldberg, like the wrestler, came up to me and said, "Where are you going?" I told him, "M an, I am going home." The next thing I know, my feet were leaving the ground, and he slammed the shit out of me. I landed on my fucking neck and couldn't breathe for what felt like forever. That was the first time I felt like I was a kid. I started scream-

---

1   The Red Dog Gang unit in Atlanta, Georgia, had a history of police brutality, violating protocol, and oppressing people. Qualified immunity allowed officers to go unpunished, contributing to systemic issues of police brutality. (Atlanta Magazine, Lisa Wilson Staff Writer, March 8, 2023)

ing for my momma, and I'm telling you if you have a hood momma, they can hear you when you scream from the street. My momma came busting out of the door and I remember thinking, *if this motherfucker puts his hands on my momma, I am going to hit another mode.*

I was on the ground and in handcuffs for the first time in my life with this grown ass man on top of me, and I had never felt that helpless in my whole life. My first reaction was, please don't pull my pants down, and he didn't. But he searched all my pockets, my book bag, and was checking my ass to see if there were drugs in there. I remember him saying, "why are you wearing a book bag?" I was coming from school, dumb motherfucker. I didn't have anything on me, and he let me go like nothing happened. From that point forward, I was going to avoid the police at all costs. But staying in the Bluff, there was no way I was going to be able to avoid them. Around this same time, they came up with some of the dumbest shit I have ever heard of called the DC-6. The cops could label areas drug zones, and you could get arrested just for standing on a corner if you're in the drug zone area. The cops could come grab you in the public bathroom, for sitting on your own porch, like whatever they felt like.[2]

Unfortunately for me, I was always so big that I was targeted all the time by the police because they thought I was older. I always worried they were going to lock me up regardless of my age. I will say that not all of the cops were bad dudes. There was a cop we called, "Action Jackson," and he was a cool dude. I don't remember his real name.

Action Jackson was one of the police officers that tried to guide me in the right direction and would talk to me sometimes. He would tell

---

2   The DC-6 refers to an ordinance that started sometime prior to March 19, 2007, when it was officially repealed. It is important to note that information about the exact start date of DC-6 is not readily available.

me to stay with the sports and go to college and get out of the area. I actually talked to him about the scholarship offer from Tennessee State, and he was supportive and that's how I met my brother Tyler!

Leaving the Bluff for College!

STREET TALES: *Bro, that is a wild story, and fortunately, we made it to TSU, brother! Do you remember when we finally met the rest of the team?*

MONTE DUNCAN: When the whole team finally got to training, I remember thinking, *these dudes are big as hell and old ass men lol.* Some of them were with me on my recruiting trip and still remembered me because, of course, we ended up getting into a fight.

For my recruiting trip, we went to a party at Fisk University. I was a recruit from Atlanta, GA, and this was the first time I had ever left my neighborhood without my mom. I remember getting picked up from the airport by some of the older guys on the team, and they got me to my hotel and shit and told me we were going out after to meet with the other recruits and the coaches.

We all met up at the hotel, and we were eating and drinking and all that stuff they do for recruits. We got to the party, and it was kind of lame. We decided to go to some club downtown. When we got to the club, the Fisk basketball team was there, and all these dudes were 6'8" and shit, and they had issues with a Tennessee State football player. A fight started and the TSU guys thought because I was a recruit I would stay back, but I was with my teammates in my mind. I jumped in and started to knock motherfuckers out.

We all got back to the cars and everyone was amped up, and they were hyping me up a little bit about getting in there with them. Not going to lie, after that experience I signed on the dotted line for Tennessee State University. I knew I wanted to play for TSU at that point because it felt familiar to me.

STREET TALES: *I will say that I did not have that same experience, but I do remember there being issues over the years with other teams, drug dealers, etc. because our teammates would be caught doing things with other dudes' girlfriends and shit lol.*

You were at Tennessee State University away from your neighborhood and your family. How did you deal with that?

MONTE DUNCAN: Tyler, I was lucky my girl pushed me do to homework and shit because I had zero interest in doing any of that. I wanted to work out and play football and education wasn't important to me. My first year, I went home after school and one of the coaches called me and said, "Boy, if you don't get your ass back here for summer school you will not play here next year." I think that's when I had to stay with you because I didn't have anywhere to go.

STREET TALES: *I remember that, I had to work all summer, and you had to go to school and shit, I don't think we ever talked about that?!*

MONTE DUNCAN: Yeah, man, I had a 1.7 GPA and that shit wasn't going to fly. I could've lost my scholarship. Coach told me that if I didn't plan on going to summer school every year that I probably wouldn't graduate. I had to struggle with that almost every year. I would just leave school and go back home and do what I was doing before. I didn't have a lot of motivation to finish school, and I never had a father figure so the coaches at TSU stepped up and motivated me to finish. I will always be thankful for that.

I think that's what motivated to go so hard on the field because I was lacking in the classroom stuff, so I would make up for it on the field. My first game at Tennessee State I got the MVP award for the John Merritt Classic. I think I intercepted the ball for a touchdown at like the 10-yard line or something and that shit stuck with me. After that game, the coach came up to me and said, "If you play like every game, then you can go home and see your son and you will be just fine here."

STREET TALES: *You were in college, you had a son in Atlanta, and if I remember correctly, your grandmother was sick?*

MONTE DUNCAN: I did have a good college career, but I wasn't fully focused on football and not focused on school. I wanted to spend more time with my son because my dad was never around, and I wasn't going to do that to my son. My grandmother was sick, and she eventually died while I was in school, and that shit hit me hard. I just wanted to drink and fight all the time.

Old Habits Die Hard, Even in College

MONTE DUNCAN: I turned into a bully, and I am not proud of that. I was 6'1" maybe 320lbs, and I would slap people in the clubs and slap their girl's ass to see if they would do anything. Nobody ever wanted to fight me or do anything to me because at that time pretty much everybody on campus knew my reputation. Then one day, I got caught slipping and a dude hit me and knocked me down. I'm not going to say I got knocked out, but I have never been knocked down before. The tables had turned. Some of our teammates jumped in and started thumping the dude until I could get out and we ran to the car. The dude followed us and started screaming that he was going to kill us. I didn't think anything of it as I have heard that so many times before and nobody ever did shit.

We drove to one of the dudes' houses, and we were chilling in the car talking about what just happened when we heard gunshots behind us and bullets were hitting the car. We were stuck in the car, so I put the seat back thinking that would save me, which was dumb. All the bullet holes were in the hood of the car, and they drove off.

I had been shot at before, so it didn't bother me too badly, but now I felt like I needed a gun. I got one from one of my homeboys before going home. I was staying at this girl's house that I was seeing and told her what happened to me. At the time, she said, "I told you to stay home. You don't need to be going out getting in trouble." She was right, but I was hardheaded.

STREET TALES: *I remember you telling me that story, but I forgot the part where you got shot at.*

MONTE DUNCAN: It gets worse. That same night, I was hungry and wanted to go to waffle house or something. I don't know why, and my girl was begging me to just stay home. My fat ass was hungry, and I wanted food, I was going out. I took one step outside of my girl's house and like ten shots rang out. I jumped back into the house and stayed my ass in the house.

After that, I ended up moving back on campus to remove myself from that situation. I didn't want to put anyone else in danger. I had a gun in my book bag every single day that year because I didn't know if the dudes were still looking for me. Long story short, we ended up running into each other again and got into a little shoot out before taking off and I never saw that dude again.

STREET TALES: *Did the police ever question you about that?*

MONTE DUNCAN: The police did question me, but it ended up being self-defense and the case was closed. I was able to move past that.

STREET TALES: *Wow, even with all that going on you were able to graduate, right?*

MONTE DUNCAN: College was not easy for me at all. But being an athlete, some females are willing to do anything for you and they helped me quite a bit so I was able to graduate!

STREET TALES: *I must ask you something before we move on to post college life. College for me was a great time, and I never had any issues with anyone at the school that I was aware of. I was told years after I graduated that there were quite a few people that had issues with me and talked about whooping my ass on or off campus. But you and some of our other teammate's kind of put the word out to the school that if anyone put hands on me that you would fuck them up?*

MONTE DUNCAN: The short answer is yes; we did do that. You were the only white guy on campus and all the cute girls wanted you even though you didn't pay them no mind. They were on your dick nonetheless. Many girls would ask me about you all the time, and it pissed a lot of dudes off, man.

STREET TALES: *I had no idea that I had this unknown protection, man. I remember we partied with all the different fraternities, the Alphas, the Q's, whatever, and I always had a good time and didn't feel the hate, I guess. It's a little late but thank you, brother!*

MONTE DUNCAN: You probably didn't know this, but me and a lot of other dudes looked up to you, man. You were married, working, smart as hell, and always seemed to have a plan for your life. Most of the hate towards you was from other dudes' because their girls were feeling you and always checking you out, and it was funny to watch because you didn't pay them any attention and probably didn't even notice it.

I am sure you didn't need any of us to fight for you as you could have kicked most of those dudes' ass anyway, but we didn't want anything to get in the way of your scholarship. You were on a minority scholarship, right?

STREET TALES: *Bro, no, I was not on a minority scholarship. Everyone always thought because I was white that I had a minority scholarship or something, which there is nothing wrong with and looking back would have been fine with me, but I was on an athletic scholarship!*

MONTE DUNCAN: That's right. You were the one who told me that white dudes could get minority scholarships to go to TSU. I remember thinking that was wild but makes sense looking back.

STREET TALES: *Switching gears a little bit, do you remember when I drove you down to Atlanta during one of our breaks to meet your mother for the first time? I walked into your house and your mother said, "I didn't know you were bringing white folks in the house."*

MONTE DUNCAN: Lol, yes, of course. You must understand, in my neighborhood we rarely see white people walking around and you were probably the first white person to ever be in our house. I had to tell her that you were my homeboy and then she was cool with it and greeted you with open arms.

There have been a lot of changes in the neighborhood, and I have white neighbors now and everything. The city is pouring money into the area and trying to make it look like downtown.

Stories From Our Time at TSU!

STREET TALES: *Couple more stories from our time together in college.*

Do you remember when we were doing walk-throughs in our team windbreakers and like five cop cars came sliding into the parking lot because someone called in saying there was a gang fight?

MONTE DUNCAN: I remember that shit and coach was trying to talk to the main cop that walked up, and we were all laughing at them and they were getting pissed.

STREET TALES: *One of the coolest things about playing for TSU, besides playing on the same field as the NFL Team, the TITANS, was playing in the B.E.T. classic every year against FAMU. I have all my jerseys from those games and still remember the feeling to this day. Playing in front of 80,000 people screaming and cheering was one of the coolest feelings of my life.*

MONTE DUNCAN: Of course, I remember that, brother. I laughed every time they gave you your jersey. The 100 Black Men's association would get us custom jerseys for each game and hand them out. Every time they got to you; they would look confused like, *this dude plays on the team.*

STREET TALES: *I still have those jerseys to this day and have them hanging up in my house!*

The last story I want to ask you about is from our freshman year in the locker room. I remember taking a shower and all the guys kept looking at me and I could feel the eyes on me. I asked you what the fuck was going on and why was everyone looking at me in the shower. You told me they had probably never seen a naked white dude before and were just curious. I got up butt naked and walked around the entire locker room so they could put their minds at ease lol! I remember everyone laughing and saying wild shit, but I never got questioned or stared at again in the locker room.

MONTE DUNCAN: Yeah, bro, because they thought you was a crazy-ass white boy walking around butt-ass naked lol. I will say, the showers in the locker room were a little crazy because you were naked with all these dudes, and I was not used to that shit at all.

STREET TALES: *You reminded me of one more story. Panera Bread and Olive Garden were two places we used to eat at all the time, probably because it was cheap or something. But you asked me what you should order, and I remember for a couple years afterwards you would call me every now and then to ask me what it was you used to order lol.*

MONTE DUNCAN: Yeah, man, because that was white people food, and I had never been to Panera Bread or Olive Garden before meeting you. I remember you opened my eyes to a lot of different shit not just food. We had wine, bourbon, and shit like that. I still don't really drink or smoke that much, but I was like fuck it, I'll try it.

It was a blessing to meet you, brother. I learned that white people aren't bad, and you showed me a bunch of shit that I might never have done if you weren't around. Black folks in Atlanta don't really hang out with white people, and it was still segregated. But now, I work in the school district and work with white people all the time, and I think it helped having met you.

STREET TALES: *What did you do when you left TSU?*

MONTE DUNCAN: I went back to Atlanta and was working for the school district when I got an offer to play for a league that was starting up. They were going to be paying $60,000 a year plus bonuses. But the league never got off the ground and they bagged out on us and never paid anyone.

Keep in mind, I had a son and daughter, and I needed to make money. I left the school, and I took out my 401K and started selling drugs. I was going back and forth from Atalanta, GA, to Knoxville, TN, and was making close to $15,000 every weekend. I was doing pretty good, and it was just me and my cousin making the runs. We were getting pretty big and making bigger runs, and I was trying to be smart by not going every weekend and mixing up the days we would go. My cousin got greedy and was making runs on his own, and he got pulled over one time with no license and $30,000 in his pocket and the police let his ass go. Another time, my cousin got pulled over and tried to run, his big ass is my size, so I don't know where he was running to. As he was running, a brick of ice (heroin) fell out of his pants. They locked his ass up, and he was looking at 20 years but ended up only getting 10 years, I believe.

He didn't tell me this at the time, and I went by myself one time and got pulled over. The cop walked up and called me Mr. Duncan. I was in a flip BMW, meaning the car was not in my name, and it hit me how the hell does he know my name? I figured our name was ringing a bell because we were getting big and had made so many runs already or something like that. When they finally got me, I was driving one of my girlfriends back home in Marietta, and I should not have been driving in Marietta. I got pulled over and had a half bag of weed on me and a small sack of sand (cocaine). They took me to county jail and told me they were going to drop the weed charges and just charge me for the cocaine. I thought I was getting a good deal but that was not the case. Because of the amount I had on me, they charged me with distribution, and I had to pay like $5,000 for a lawyer and another $3,000 to the court and it drained me. Altogether, I ended up getting probation and I think that was the best thing that could have happened to me in my life because I slowed down and only fucked with weed and left that hard shit alone.

I thank God that I didn't get locked up and sent away, and it gave me clarity to stop doing what I was doing and be there for my kids. I was selfish man and could have gotten locked up and left my kids with nothing and no father. I had to let that shit go and do what I had to do to provide for them.

STREET TALES: *What are you doing now?*

MONTE DUNCAN: I work at Tri-City High School in Atlanta, GA. I am athletic custodian and deal with the fields and things like that. I want to do something that people can respect, like, *he is providing for his family and doing honest work.*

STREET TALES: *I appreciate you, brother, and you're doing the right thing and with your personality and work ethic. I know you make an impact on everyone you work with and come across.*

Story Wrap Up

I consider Monte to be one of my close friends. His upbringing was vastly different than mine, and yet we had and still have comradery via our shared experiences. Monte was put in a bad situation at an early age, and I truly believe he made the best out of an otherwise dangerous and volatile situation. Even with all the violence, disappointment, and negative interactions with the world around him, he is a good man, a good father, and owns up to his mistakes and moves on. Monte didn't allow his childhood and subsequent stint in jail define who he would be for life.

Monte has a solid hold of his core values and is willing to put his life on the line to defend those values. Monte is just one example of not taking on a victim mentality and allowing that to dictate the goals of your life, regardless of the nature of your surroundings.

The Story of Monte Duncan

Click or scan the QR Code
to hear the podcast interview

with **Dave Tarbox**

The Story of
DAVE TARBOX

D ave Tarbox and I met at a barber shop in Falmouth, Maine, and we have known each other for many years. For those of you who have ever gone into a barbershop, you have conversations with each other about work, sports, politics, crypto, and a hundred other things. I have always tried to develop a good relationship with my barbers over the years as they can make or break a haircut.

I remember when Dave asked me what I did for work, and I told him I was a Special Agent for the United States Secret Service. There is the inevitable bullshit meter followed by "really?" Dave was nothing but supportive and thought it was a cool job and would ask lots of questions. I can't remember what led to Dave talking about his criminal past, but when he did, the barbershop got a little quieter and I could tell they were waiting on my reaction. I asked a few questions but otherwise did not put much weight into the conversation at the time. I didn't care about what he used to do and only cared about what he was doing now.

When Dave opened his own shop, I followed him because as most people know, when you find a good barber, you stick with that barber! That's when we began having more detailed conversations about his life and his experiences. I found his story fascinating and asked if he would speak at various high schools with me. Dave agreed and the combo of Dave and I was awesome. Dave is a great speaker and so honest with his perspective on what he was doing and what led to him being in prison.

"I was arrested for eight bank robberies and convicted on four bank robberies; I've robbed more banks than Jesse James." (One of my favorite lines from listening to Dave speak!)

One of the main things Dave focuses on is to not glamorize crime or drugs, and when you speak with him, you can tell that he has accepted that part of his life but has moved on and has become a successful business owner, a father, and a great friend.

Below is a conversation with Dave Tarbox and I:

FROM CHAOS TO CLARITY:
The Redemption of Dave Tarbox

STREET TALES: *I have my friend, Dave Tarbox, on today! Dave has one of the wildest life stories I have ever heard! He is open and honest and, in my opinion, sheds a raw and humble insight into drug addiction, the criminal mind, and rehabilitation and redemption.*

DAVE TARBOX: Thanks, Tyler, appreciate it, man. This is humbling to say the least coming from the exact opposite side of law enforcement. I don't get asked to do stuff like this every day, and it's a cool opportunity. I appreciate it.

I met Tyler a few years ago, and we hit it off pretty much instantly.

We got to talking and got into each other's backstories over the course of a year or so and got to know each other. I'm from Massachusetts, just south of Boston, Quincy originally, bounced around a lot as a kid and I never really fit in. I moved to Maine a few years ago and that's where I became a barber. When I was young, I never lived in one area long enough to make a core group of friends till I got to high school. It was easy enough to fall in with the fuck-ups because you just had to act up in class and the kids who were acting up in class were like, "Hey, he's one of us." You could go down the park, you could smoke a cigarette, and the kids that were down the park smoking cigarettes were like, "Hey, he's one of us." I never had to wait to be accepted by those guys. I didn't play sports or anything like that as a kid.

Later on in life, that led me to drugs and then drugs led me to a life of crime for a number of years. Through trial and error, I eventually was able to turn my life around, and it's kind of where I'm at right now and I'm pretty grateful for that.

STREET TALES: *Yeah, Dave, I think we kind of have different paths that we've taken, our growing up, our childhood. I did have sports. My dad got me into sports when I was eight years old, but I grew up in the projects in Atlanta where I was usually the only white kid.*

There's a story I have with my mom involving the kids in the neighborhood, because I was one of the only white kids. My mom was a Marine, so she didn't make a lot of money. I was coming home from the school bus and kids started throwing rocks at me and they hit me in the face. One hit me right between the eyes. I still have the scar from it. I was bleeding all down my face and my mom thought I had actually gotten shot.

I kind of bounced around, and I was kind of in the same boat as you, got kicked out of preschool. It was rough and I appreciate the struggle

41

that my mother had and my dad, because they separated, but Marines aren't well paid. We were always in a trailer park or the hood or whatever.

I bounced around a lot as well between the two of them. I would say the difference I had was that I did have sports. Sports kind of gave me an immediate injection of friends and kept me moving down the right path. Not that I didn't get into some weed and stuff when I was in high school, but that's a little different.

Early Life

DAVE TARBOX: The first time I got drunk I was like seven years old. I was drawn to that lifestyle. I saw it as I emulated adults or people who I thought were adults. I thought that's how I was supposed to act. Even at a very young age, I was trying to play this part. I feel like I created a lot of my problems myself looking back on it now. But you know, that's what I wanted. It's really hard to tell a kid, who knows everything, that they're fucking up.

STREET TALES: *Yeah, I've seen it. I don't know that I could necessarily speak from experience on it. You said you bounced around a lot. Do you have anywhere that you specifically call home?*

DAVE TARBOX: My mother went back to nursing school, and she ended up buying a house in Whitman, Mass. When I was in high school, we moved out of Quincy. We went from Quincy to Braintree. I spent a lot of time at my grandparents' house in Weymouth. Then my grandparents ended up moving down the Cape. I would spend summers down there with them. Basically, I'm from the South Shore of Massachusetts, Boston South. I lived in Boston for a little while. When we moved out of Quincy, my parents wanted to get away from the city hoping to keep me out of trouble. But when we moved to Whitman, next to Whitman is Brockett. I was drawn to it. I was like, ooh, what's this? A 20-minute walk down the street, and we're right back to it.

STREET TALES: *I could tell you one story about Brockton that I had with the Cape Verdean president and their prime minister. This was when I was working for the Secret Service.*

DAVE TARBOX: They go there to campaign because Cape Verdeans can still vote in national elections. They go to the high school all the time. That's a big-ass high school too, huh?[3]

STREET TALES: *We rolled in and I was relatively new and I was actually driving that time. The cops were like, "Do you guys know where you are? What are you doing?" We were at the consulate or*

---

3   There are more Cape Verdeans in Brockton, Massachusetts than there are in Cape Verde itself. Cape Verde is a chain of small islands off the coast of Senegal, Africa. Politicians will go to Brockton, MA, when they are campaigning or when there is important legislation to garner votes. The Cape Verdeans in Brockton, MA are allowed to vote in elections in Cape Verde even when living in the United States of America.

When I worked for the United States Secret Service, we would typically protect the President or Prime Minister as they share power and will campaign together. Their staff and security detail were always very professional and worked well with the Secret Service agents assigned to protect them.

church or something. I don't remember what they called it. It's not really an embassy. The cop said, "We just had two shootings here a few hours ago. We'll do the best we can, but we need you guys to understand where you're at." I was thinking holy crap.

The people themselves that were there were great. We had a great time and the food was amazing. It was interesting. There's more Cape Verdeans in Brockton than there are on Cape Verde.

I started my Secret Service Career in Boston, and I didn't realize how big of a role Boston PD, Mass. State Police are. They're powerhouses in New England. I'm assuming you had interactions with them growing up.

DAVE TARBOX: Yeah, I saw law enforcement a little bit. When I started fucking off, I really started fucking off. Most of my arrests were by the Mass. state police. They have a large drug task force and gang task forces. Those are the type of people that I would have run into just because I was based in the areas like Brockton. There was something like a DEA Brockton police state task force.

The task forces were attempting to cut down on the gang crime and the drug crime and stuff like that. But because I was in those types of neighborhoods, that's just who I was running into.

You Don't Need an ID to Buy Drugs

STREET TALES: *I definitely get it. Mass. State Police, I mean, it's wild working with law enforcement all over the country. Mass. police, there's like 3000. I don't know if it's troopers or people, but for state police that's massive. When I worked for Main State Police, they had 243 state troopers for the entire state of Maine.*

You said you started fucking off and then really fucking off, what age range was that?

DAVE TARBOX: I was a heroin addict at 17. I was shooting dope like an adult when I was a kid. I didn't even know how to wash my ass properly. You know what I mean? I had no idea what I was doing. It took a couple of years to really catch up with me because at that age, people didn't expect me to be a drug addict. I still was able to get jobs, and I was still able to support myself. I would say early twenties is when my life like really started falling apart. That's when I started getting arrested, became homeless, and I really let drugs consume me. I started selling drugs, but like the majority of drug dealers, especially the ones that I knew, I was just selling drugs to support my habit.

STREET TALES: *What got you into heroin originally? Because that is a pretty hardcore drug to start off with or use at such a young age?*

DAVE TARBOX: I would say I started smoking weed and drinking, smoking cigarettes in junior high school, but when you're that young, you really can't get stuff like that. However, I did start hanging out with older kids, and they were able to get stuff. We hung out down at the park and people would have their dime bags of weed and be drinking beers. It was easy enough to follow that group of people, and there were some good guys, some people I'm still friends with today, but for the most part, we were fucking off and we were fucked up. Around freshman year of high school, we got introduced to Oxys. By sophomore year, that was really our flavor, Oxys.

Again, we didn't know what we were doing, and we were just doing them all the time. The problem was it was easier for us to get that than it was to get beer. You know what I mean? To get beer was a multi-step process. We had to get the money. We had to find somebody that was 21, and we would have to have a ride. You don't have to have an ID to buy drugs.

STREET TALES: *I never thought about that way.*

DAVE TARBOX: At the time, a lot of pharmacies were getting robbed. Before then, the drugs were dirt cheap. They were handing them out. You'd have like four guys; everybody threw in like five or 10 bucks. You got on the street, buy an 80, split it and you'd all be rocked for the whole night.

I started doing that a couple nights a week. Then as the robberies started happening, the prices started going up because they started getting harder and harder to get. As the prices started going up, we started getting introduced more and more to heroin. At first, it was a once in a while thing. You really have to go out of your way to find it. By the time I was about 17, it was commonplace, and it was a fraction of the price.

At that time, Oxys had gone up from like $20 to probably $60 a piece when you could get it. You could get like half a gram of heroin for like 30 bucks and that kept you high for two days. The problem is, the dependence on heroin goes up quickly too. What starts as maybe like a $15 a day habit, you know, months and years later, it's a couple hundred dollars a day and it's just unsustainable.

STREET TALES: *Do you think heroin is worse than the oxy itself? I've never actually asked that question.*

DAVE TARBOX: The kick from OxyContin, because it's made in the lab, it's engineered to be super pure and super effective. When that shit gets into you like that, it's medicine. It gets into your bones; it gets into your muscles. It's a terrible kick. Not that heroin is any easier, but I feel like it just lasted. The withdrawals from the OxyContin were drawn out.

STREET TALES: *Well, I know we're probably going to jump around a little bit, but when was the first time you went through a withdrawal? I've heard people die from it.*

DAVE TARBOX: I don't remember how old I was, maybe like 16, 17 years old. I was working for this company delivering party supplies and I was pulling a dolly through this guy's backyard and I was like, "I think I've got a cold." I was talking to the kid I was working with and I said, "It's like the flu. I'm congested. My nose is running. My stomach's all messed up. My bones and joints are all achy." The kid said, "You've been fucking with them pills, haven't you? That's what it is." I asked him what he was talking about. "You're having withdrawal, dude. You're jonesing and you're going to go get high." I was like, "No, man, I'm not fucking addicted." That sat in the back of my head for a couple of hours. I got home, went and got a pill, got high, and it went away. I was fucking dope sick. Like, that's why I felt like that. I thought, *well, let's not let that happen again.*

Instead of thinking, *shit, I gotta get away from this.* I was like, *shit, I need to get more of this so that doesn't happen again.*

STREET TALES: *That started around 17. You said 20s was when it kind of started taking off for you on the criminal side and homelessness. I actually I don't think you and I have ever talked about the homelessness side, but what were you doing? I'm assuming this was to feed the addiction.*

DAVE TARBOX: My parents picked up on the fact that something was going on. My brother and my father are also drug addicts. I'm not going to speak on their situation. I only say that because it runs in the family, and it was more accepted in my household. I didn't really hide things from my parents. They knew to a certain extent what was going on. They didn't know I was sticking needles in my arm when I was that young, but they knew that I was into some shit.

Once they realized what was going on, they were like, "Bro, you got to go." "Really?" "Yeah, like you can't be doing this shit around the house." At the time I was dating this girl, so I would kind of stay at her place. I kind of cleaned up my act a little bit.

My parents let me come back to the house but not right away. I lived in Brockton for a couple of years when I was around 22, and everybody was like, "Bro, we're fucking sick of you. When you come around here, the chain goes missing, the roaches are gone from the ashtray; so, don't come around here no more." I had burned all my bridges at that point. At one point, I actually lived in my girlfriend's car. I didn't even have my own car. I lived in her car for about a year and then I ended up totaling that car.

My First Love & First Time Going to Jail

STREET TALES: *When was your first stint in jail?*

DAVE TARBOX: I was living in Brockton with my girl, and it was a rocky relationship, and I wasn't allowed to stay with her anymore. She would let me sleep in the car that was parked in front of her house sometimes.

When I met this girl, I had a short period of sobriety and was staying with my parents again. I had signed up for some classes at a local community college, figured education was the way to turn my life around. I met her when I was 20 or 21 and she was 18. She had just gotten out of high school, and we started dating. She was just starting the party scene, so she was drinking and doing drugs. When I started to introduce harder things like cocaine and pills, it wasn't that crazy to her. It started out as a once in a while thing for me, but since I am an addict, it progressed quickly, and she was keeping up but registered the change in me first. This went on for almost five years, and we went through some shit together before I finally went to prison for bank robbery, and we went our separate ways.

STREET TALES: *That was the final straw for her?*

DAVE TARBOX: No, that wasn't the final straw for her, we talked for a couple years into my prison sentence and exchanged letters and stuff like that. We would talk on the phone every once in a while, and she would talk to my family on birthdays and holidays. But I had to go in a different direction and separate myself from the lifestyle, so I went one way, and she went another.

STREET TALES: *I understand, and again I apologize for jumping around, but do you remember your first arrest and what that was for?*

DAVE TARBOX: My first arrest was an assault and battery charge with my girl's father. Her father liked to drink and run his mouth. I was sitting in front of his house while my girl was inside speaking with her mother about something, I don't remember. We didn't like each other, and when he came home and saw me hanging out in front of his house, he was pissed and already drunk. He went upstairs and said something to my girl and her mother then came outside and started talking shit to me while I was sitting in the car. I ran my mouth back to him and he hit me. I got out of the car, and we started fighting and tossing each other in the street. My girl came outside and was trying to break it up, and he hit her and then all bets were off. I felt like he hit her on purpose.

I was in a full rage, and when the fight was over, he ended up going to the hospital and her mother called the police. I took off and that was a mistake because he was able to tell his version of the story, which made it look like I was hiding under the stairs and attacked him when he came home.

STREET TALES: *Yeah, unfortunately, I know exactly what you are talking about, and I have seen shit like that happen a few times in my law enforcement career. Cops have to kind of pick a side and that is unfortunate.*

DAVE TARBOX: He had lived in Brockton his whole life and has a big Irish family so he knew a lot of people, and it makes sense they would believe his version of the story. Also, if I wasn't such a scumbag and put myself in that situation, it never would have happened.

STREET TALES: *Like I said earlier, I have seen shit like that happen. When I was a Deputy in Hillsborough County, FL, I met a guy who* *had been convicted of multiple felonies all stimming from domestic violence charges. I arrested him a few times and asked him about it one time and he advised he has ten "baby mammas" and can't afford child support. He would get into arguments and sometimes it was violent and sometimes it wasn't, but he was always the one to get arrested. Then there would be a protection order against him, but he wanted to see his kids, and their mothers would want money and shit. He would try to see his kids and give what money he could with the understanding he was invited there. Inevitably the cops would be called, and he would get arrested again for violating the protection order and it was a vicious cycle.*

Also, in the state of Florida, if you don't pay your child support, your license can be suspended. After being stopped/caught three times driving on a suspended license, it becomes a felony. He had numerous felony arrests stemming from driving on a suspended license due to lack of child support. This man was caught in a horrible cycle where he could not drive to work because his license was suspended and could not see his children due to all the protection orders. I had no advice and could not even begin to figure out a way to help this man get out of his situation.

DAVE TARBOX: When I would speak to the kids in the high schools, I would tell them that once you get caught up in the system, it is hard to get out of it. The judicial system is not set up to help you get back on the right path, and I was not educated at all prior to getting caught up in a life of crime. I would always tell the kids that they need to be educated before taking any deals or speaking to cops, lawyers, and hopefully, they never have to speak to a judge, but life happens.

Feeding the Drug Habit

STREET TALES: *I couldn't agree more with educating yourself! We checked off the first arrest and we have teased the bank robbery charge a few times, but what led up to you eventually robbing your first bank?*

DAVE TARBOX: Like I said, the last couple years, things were getting progressively worse for me, and I was doing stupid things and getting arrested for them. I got picked up on shoplifting charges and drug possession, stupid stuff like that. As I mentioned, I was not educated on the system and would go in front of a judge and the judge would say, "Sign this piece of paper and plead guilty and you can leave today." I would get six months of unsupervised probation or whatever the case might be. I was like hell yeah, whatever I can do to get out of here I would do! But then I would get arrested for driving without a license or failing a drug test, and the unsupervised probation would turn into supervised probation and so on and so forth.

Also, my drug habit was just ramping out of control, and I was trying to sell drugs to support a habit. I would try to work when I could work and was pulling off a little nickel here or a dime there. I was just doing the most basic criminal shit to eke by, and it was a miserable existence. I was doing all of this to fuel my drug habit, and the crimes kept escalating to support the ever-growing drug use. I got arrested a few times with heroine on me or crack, and it was getting worse and worse for me.

I started to get sick of the low-level criminal shit like ripping off construction sites, stealing a car, taking tools, trying to pawn stuff. The people I was running around with were not professional criminals or anything like that. We would link up and just try to figure out what we could steal at night and sell to get enough money to support that day/night's drug use. There was one day I got arrested for shoplifting twice in the same day, and I think that was the turning point for me to stop doing petty shit and figure out a way to make real money.

Since I needed money, I figured the most direct line to money was banks. Typically, when you steal something, even if it has a high value, the people you sell it to try to give you the least amount of money possible for the item and it's bullshit. I wanted money, I didn't want to have to steal something, then get money from someone else and I didn't want to get caught stealing something that again I would have to find someone to buy. Too many chances to get caught when you are selling stolen shit to people.

So, I started passing notes to rob banks.

STREET TALES: *Can we address your drug habit for just a minute? You said you were taking eighty milligrams of oxycontin each day at a young age, so I am assuming it only got worse from there?*

DAVE TARBOX: By the end of high school, I was primarily doing oxycontin and would dabble with heroin. The oxys were a big thing on construction sites as a lot of those guys would get injured or just through wear and tear on their bodies started taking oxys to get through the day.

I was 17 working on job sites with guys who were in their 30's and 40's doing pain pills. They would either be taking the pain pills or selling the pain pills, and it was just an accepted part of the job site.

It was common to take a pain pill in the morning and again in the afternoon, and at the end of the day smoke a joint and have a couple drinks. The pain pills were more accepted than taking heroin, and that stuff was still super underground. I had a lot of friends whose first felony was getting caught with hypodermic syringes at like 19 years old. Now they are selling heroin and making runs to Rhode Island to buy syringes. They didn't sell syringes in Massachusetts at the time, and you had to have a prescription for them or be part of an exchange program. It wasn't like it is today where people just do it in the open and you see it everywhere.

STREET TALES: *I have one more side question before we start talking about the bank robberies and I am not asking you to incriminate yourself, but did you ever successfully steal a car and convert that into money?*

DAVE TARBOX: I'm going to take some liberties with my stories and exaggerate the names and places to protect the guilty. One night, I went out with one of my boys and we decided we were going to steal a car and hit a major fucking lift the next day. We wouldn't have to worry about getting caught because we would be in a stolen car. We scraped together like eight dollars and some loose cigarettes, and we were looking for 1998 Honda Civic because someone had taught us how to steal that specific car like ten years earlier. It was funny because I remember it had to be blue and a hatchback because that was the only one we knew how to hotwire. We ended up driving around Boston for most of the day and finally found what we were looking for behind a train station. We stole the car and dumped it behind an apartment complex with plans to get it in the morning.

Surprisingly, the car was still there in the morning, and we were going to use it to steal tools and shit from Home Depot or something like that. My job was to be the driver, and my buddy was going to go into the Home Depot and steal the tools and shit. I remember laughing at him because he was all dressed up in business casual with a button up shirt lol. He had the tie pulled down a little bit, khaki pants that were way too big for him and a busted pleat with some brown loafers. He felt like it was his undercover look or something, I don't know, but it was ridiculous looking back at it. He went into the store and filled up a carriage with power tools and stuff and walked up to the front door and left the carriage before walking out. He got into the car and said that he can't do it. We stole a car the night before for no reason, and I think we even took the car back to where we stole it.

I only ever stole cars to go commit other crimes in and shit. I never knew where the chop shops were, and I am not a mechanic, I never figured out how to convert stealing cars into money. I wish back then I could've figured it out, but it never got to that level for me.

STREET TALES: *I arrested a dude in Florida who used to steal eighteen wheelers and large construction equipment back in the day. He would steal them from Tampa, FL and run them to Miami, FL for several years. He told me he would steal equipment that cost a hundred thousand dollars and would be lucky if he got twenty thousand dollars for his trouble.*

DAVE TARBOX: There were rumors of one place in Boston, and it was kind of like what you are describing. Like I mentioned before, there is a large immigrant population in Mass., and it's hard for them to get high-end items so they would break stuff down and send it back home, wherever that might be. I did have a couple drug dealers over the years that took stolen credit cards and big screen TVs as payment. They would also give you a fraction of the actual price for the items, but that's how those things go.

Interactions with Law Enforcement

STREET TALES: *Through all the arrests over the years, do any troopers or cops stand out for being super cool or a fucking asshole?*

DAVE TARBOX: There were several cops that probably saw the writing on the wall for me and what I was doing when I was younger and they would bust my balls, for all the right reasons. But when you're a teenager and you're driving around drinking beers and doing dumb shit, you're like *why can't I do whatever I want? Those cops are fucking pricks*, but that's just kids doing and thinking dumb shit.

There was one guy, Sgt. Bates, who is an amazing human being and treated me well considering the circumstances. Ofc. Pearson was another great guy and I went to high school with his daughters. Ofc. Pearson would always try to speak into my life and ask me what the fuck was I doing lol.

I didn't make it easy when dealing with law enforcement as I was usually disheveled and I was a scumbag committing crimes. Their job is to stop people like me from wreaking havoc in their towns. I mean, people are trying to work and run a business, and they shouldn't have to worry about their tools being stolen off job sites and other things going missing because of people like me. From my perspective, they were doing what they were supposed to do, and I was doing what I was supposed to do.

STREET TALES: *That reminds of a guy I arrested in Tampa, FL, who was a professional shoplifter and was hitting all the Walmart's in the area. He had shopping lists that he would work off of while stealing large quantities of items. When we tried to question him,*

I'll never forget his response, "I ain't got shit to say to you. I've been doing this shit since 1983! You do your job and I'll do my job."

I've Robbed More Banks Than Jesse James

DAVE TARBOX: When I finally got arrested for the bank robberies, I was back in Massachusetts, and it's a very formal procedure when the FBI interviews you. They have all the brass and cameras setup with three guys in suits sitting across from you. They come in and they go through this whole spiel, "I am special agent in charge so-and-do, and this is special agent whoever and that's detective so-and-so. The time is 17:04 and 13 seconds. We are going to ask you some questions about pending federal bank robbery charges." I responded, "You're gonna have to talk to my lawyer."

STREET TALES: *Let's get into the story of how you got into robbing banks all the way to heading to prison.*

DAVE TARBOX: I was what is known as a note passer. I would go into a bank and grab a withdraw slip and I would write on the withdraw slip *give me the fucking money* or something like that. A couple times the bank tellers would laugh and ask, "Is this a joke?" I would respond, "No. Give me the fucking money," and they would typically give me the money, and I would leave.

STREET TALES: *Would you mask up or try to hide your identity or anything?*

DAVE TARBOX: At the time, I looked like a homeless guy, long hair, disheveled clothing, etc. I would wear a hat or a hoodie, something like that to hide my face as much as I could but never a mask or anything. I never wanted to wear a mask and have guns blazing or anything like that. I wanted to get an amount of money and get out the door as fast as I could.

STREET TALES: *Do you remember the first bank you robbed and how much you got?*

DAVE TARBOX: I do. It was really scary, and I was pretty young when I did that, and I got a lot of money, almost $10,000. I got hooked pretty quickly as there is not much work you can do and make $8,000 to $10,000 for an hour of work.

STREET TALES: *What did you do with the money? Was the habit so strong at that point that you spent it quickly or did you try to kick money to people?*

DAVE TARBOX: That's the thing. You spend the money almost as quickly as you get the money. When I was selling drugs, I would sell enough to buy more stuff and just barely scrape by. With the banks, I went from living in a car to living in hotels every night, which is a couple hundred dollars a night cause you're not going to go to the motel down the street or anything like that. We would usually smoke crack and stay in the Copley Place in Boston for a few nights.

STREET TALES: *Was $10,000 the biggest score?*

DAVE TARBOX: No, one time I got $15,000, but typically, it was much less than $10,000 and sometimes as low as $1,500. The $15,000 hit was different as I remember the bank teller acting like it was her money and even said something to that effect. It's not your fucking money; you're still going to get a paycheck at the end of the week.

I also thought the note passing was a victimless crime, but then I got the discovery packet, and it had witness statements in it. One of the women that I had passed the note to wrote that she was having a hard time going back to work because she was so scared and always looking over her shoulder. At the time I remember thinking, "I can't' believe this bitch." She is trying to get workman's comp because of me and scam the system. It hit me years later that I fucked up that lady's day and maybe her life. I didn't realize how the note passing was affecting people, and it was a fucked-up thing to do.

STREET TALES: *Obviously, this is all from the past and people who know you now would be shocked, in my opinion. You're a good man, a father, and a successful businessman now. Most of that comes from your personality, and I can only imagine how hard this story is for you and what you did.*

Switching gears, without incriminating yourself, how many banks did you do this to over the years?

Life of Crime Comes to an End

DAVE TARBOX: I was arrested for eight bank robberies and convicted on four. I'm going to say that I robbed more than two and less than 10. *I've robbed more banks than Jesse James.*

STREET TALES: *Fair enough. Let's talk about what actually got you arrested as that was in the news, and I've read the article, but I want to talk about it from your perspective.*

DAVE TARBOX: I was at a hotel partying after passing a note at a bank and my phone started ringing and when I picked it up a voice said, "I saw you on the news and it's definitely you. You need to cut that shit out," then hung up. I turned on the news and there I was. I figured, *Okay, I need to get out of here and lay low for a while.* What I had been doing since I was 19 years old, was any time I made a large score I would disappear to New York and lay low there as long as the money lasted. I was in NY when the news broke about my last few robberies, and my plan was to go to Louisiana around the Gulf Coast and work on an oil rig or find some construction site.

STREET TALES: *How far did you make it before getting arrested?*

DAVE TARBOX: I got arrested in Raleigh, NC by the United States Marshalls at a bus station. It was kind of fun to be honest. I was tweaked out of my mind, and I believe someone from the bus station called the police because I was smoking crack in the little bathroom on the bus while we were driving down the highway, Jesus, man.

I got off the bus to use the restroom, and as I was walking down the hallway to the bathroom, there were two guys in there and I could tell something was off as soon as I walked in there. I thought I had interrupted a blow job or something. The vibe was really weird in the bathroom.

I remember stopping at the vending machine before going into the bathroom because I saw these cookies that they sell in the prison commissary and thought it might be a bad omen to buy prison cookies, but they are so good, so I bought them.

Anyway, the two guys in the bathroom were undercover cops or something and they followed me out of the bathroom and scooped me up. I was walking down this hallway, and two dudes as big as you, you know 6'3" or 6'4", threw me up against the wall and started yelling at me. They kept asking me where the gun was. I guess someone told them I had a gun which I didn't, and they just kept yelling at me, "Where's the gun?"

They ended up searching the bus and did not find a gun, but they found my drugs and some drug paraphernalia. The drug laws in North Carolina are different than the laws in Massachusetts so the cops were like, "You're smoked, dude. We have you dead to rights." In my head I was like, *these drug charges are the least of my worries lol.*

I did not fight extradition back to Massachusetts, which I could have but I just wanted to get this all over with. I was relieved, to be honest, that it was all over.

STREET TALES: *How did they transport you from North Carolina to Massachusetts?*

DAVE TARBOX: I was picked up by this husband-and-wife team in a Jeep Cherokee actually. They drove me to Texas because they had to drop off another prisoner before driving me up to Massachusetts. We would drive for like eight hours or something, and then they would drop me at the county jail before picking me up in the morning.

When I finally got to the jail, I was told they were charging me with eight bank robberies but when all was said and done, they only indicted me for four bank robberies and I ended up getting a five-year prison sentence.

STREET TALES: *What was your take on your defense attorney?*

DAVE TARBOX: Actually, a funny story, I was in Fall River Courthouse and they had just opened a New Superior Courthouse at the time. I will say, you meet some of the funniest people ever in jails. It must be from the trauma, like everyone's life sucks and they are miserable. The shit that comes out of people's mouths is gold lol. This guy came off the elevator and I heard somebody yell, "Oh, shit, look at this motherfucker in a bow tie. Somebody going to jail for a long ass time!"

I got up to see who they were talking about and who this idiot was, and I heard him ask, "Are you Mr. Tarbox?" Fuck me! I will say again, you have to educate yourself on the system and know that you can fire your assigned defense attorney. I would have fired him for sure and done my best to get another attorney. But I was naïve of the system, and he was an older gentleman, and he was court appointed, so I assumed he was good.

Looking back, I could tell he was just going through the motions, and I got five years. I will say in his defense, that he had the charges dropped from eight banks to four banks so, he basically cut my sentence in half. I will give him that. The prosecutors were looking to sentence me for 10 to 12 years, and I ended up with five.

My defense attorney was able to use the fruit of the poisonous tree to get some of the banks off the indictment. The investigators used a picture of me robbing a bank to get a positive identification from another bank.

STREET TALES: *Did you end up in federal prison?*

DAVE TARBOX: I went to state prison actually, and the way it was explained to me was the sentencing guidelines are basically the same. So they charged me under state charges instead of federal charges. Looking back at everything, I realized the feds only like to prosecute slam-dunk cases, and they had some shaky identification and realized there might be a bit of wiggle room, so they left it in state courts. They did tell me that if I ever got arrested for something else that it would more than likely end up in Federal Court.

STREET TALES: *What was your moment of clarity to turn your life around?*

DAVE TARBOX: The first big moment of clarity was about 10 months in when I learned I was going to get moved upstate to another prison. So like any good con will do, I sold some shit and bought some crack.

I was in my cell smoking crack in my jail uniform laying under my bunk with my ass out all tweaked out. I could feel eyes on me and I wiggled out from under my bunk and there was a jail guard standing there staring at me. It's like two o'clock in the morning so I jumped back into my bunk and tried to act like I am sleeping. I was laying there and thinking to myself, *what are you doing, man? You're in jail and you're still smoking crack, are you enjoying yourself?*

That's when I started to clean myself up and stopped trying to get in trouble. It was not easy and I used a few more times. But overall, I wanted to get my life together.

When I got out, I used again and started hanging out with the same people and same shitty relationship. I moved out of Massachusetts to get some space, like a geographical cure, to get away from the life I had always known. I didn't want that life anymore.

Redemption

STREET TALES: *I met you at a barbershop in Falmouth, Maine. When did you become a barber and how did all of that come to pass?*

DAVE TARBOX: Shout out to the boys at Americana! I apprenticed under Jake when he owned the barbershop. They started in Portland, ME, and then moved the shop to Falmouth, ME, and I followed them to the store in Falmouth. I have nothing but respect and appreciation for the boys at Americana. They taught me everything I needed to know and helped get me back on the right track.

I was commuting to Falmouth from Biddeford, ME, and my great friend, Dre, and I decided to open our own barbershop in Biddeford. We opened Gentlemen's Studio Barbering a few years back and things have been going great! We have been doing what we can to become part of the community and grow our business.

STREET TALES: *Last time I was there you had people lined up and now you have cop buddies, and they are clients of yours!*

DAVE TARBOX: My ex's uncle is a retired police officer up here and Maine is a small community, so, you really must rely on word of mouth and make sure you're doing good work! I will say the guys that come into the shop are a great group of guys and their support means a lot to me and Dre.

STREET TALES: *Honestly, you're a good person and have great work ethic. I remember you were telling me you were working like 18-hour days getting the shop ready and doing most of the work yourselves. Add all of that to your story and you have something special, brother. You're a success story, and it's still getting better!*

DAVE TARBOX: I said that to myself when I was in prison. I had done a couple of skid bids up until that point and know I was doing years. I would see fellow inmates just give up and they would change. I never wanted that to happen to me. I never had a victim mentality, and I wasn't going to start then. When I would talk to people, they would say their parents are shitty or the system did them wrong and "that's why I am in here." I didn't think like that, and eventually, I figured out a path for my life.

STREET TALES: *Well, thank God you did, bro, because you have helped so many people, including me and my son.*

We also used to go speak at high schools together about law enforcement and the other side of law enforcement. I don't know what you said exactly to the kids, but they absolutely loved it and always requested you come back!

DAVE TARBOX: I was just honest with them!

Story Wrap Up

Unfortunately, Dave Tarbox's story is not unique in Massachusetts, but he is able to articulate his struggle from a unique perspective. Dave grew up in a low socioeconomic area and at an early age was attracted to the destructive side of adult behavior. Dave explains why he was attracted to the behavior, and throughout his story, you can begin to understand how addiction can start and eventually takeover your life.

It is amazing to me that Dave was able to keep maintain a positive attitude and not succumb to a victim or helpless mentality. Through his own hard work and dedication to his family and his friends, Dave has rebuilt his future from something dark and destructive into a thriving business and is able to provide his children a stable home and father figure.

The Story of Dave Tarbox

Click or scan the QR Code
to hear the podcast interview

with **Joe Caputo**

The Story of
JOE CAPUTO

oe Caputo and I met a few years ago because our girlfriends at the time felt we should meet each other. As any man knows, this is not usually the most ideal scenario to make a friend lol. Joe is a large dude, extremely fit, and in executive sales. I was immediately suspicious. Joe is one of the best examples of not judging a book by its cover. Here is a man who is fit and a successful salesman and business owner but is also humble, open, and well-spoken. It was the humility and openness that bridged the initial uncomfortable getting-to-know-each-other phase.

I tend to stay to myself and never really go out of my way to make "new" friends, so to speak. But with Joe it was different, and he was very comfortable speaking about a wide range of topics, including his personal life. Joe is an addict. Such a short sentence but a powerful one nonetheless. Over the years we have known each other, Joe has shared his early drug addiction and a short stint in criminality. His addiction was so severe that he overdosed not once but twice! The second overdose was the one that rocked him to his core and created a drive to change the trajectory of his life:

"I was lying there, barely conscious, listening to my 'friends' discuss how to get rid of my body."

Joe decided that this was not how he was going to die and set off on a path that led to hundreds of pounds of weight loss and an extremely successful business career. We have become close friends, and I value his insight and experience in many aspects of my life. Joe has one of the craziest stories of addiction, crime, willpower, and redemption that I have ever heard. Joe's ability to be introspective at such a young age and to make life altering changes is inspiring, and I cannot thank him enough for sharing his story with me!

Joe met me at The Village, a legendary recording studio in Los Angeles, CA to record his story:

TURNING PAST STRUGGLES INTO FUEL FOR SUCCESS
with Joe Caputo

STREET TALES: *I have my friend, Joe Caputo, here today and he's got a fucking phenomenal life story. I'm not going to overhype it right now, but, Joe, I appreciate you being here, brother.*

JOE CAPUTO: Yeah, absolutely, brother, appreciate the time.

I know we've been talking about doing this for a while. Now we are out here in beautiful LA at The Village Studios.

This studio is absolutely amazing. As you know, last year I was doing a podcast for a period of time and then stopped that to just focus on other stuff. So, this is a great kickoff, kind of motivating me to get back into it.

STREET TALES: *Right, dude? Yeah, shake the cobwebs out a little bit. Do you mind describing the studio? Because I've tried to describe the studio to various people and I clearly do a terrible job capturing the vibe and the history that is here.*

JOE CAPUTO: I mean, from the aspect of when you say studio, most people think of like all the kind of pop-up podcasts studios, right? That's actually how I record mine. Nothing wrong with it. But this studio is legitimately a professional music studio. I mean, one of the things that caught my eye right when I walked in the door was fucking a track for Dr. Dre and just plaques all over the wall.

STREET TALES: *It's still a super chill, laid-back vibe in here and it's phenomenal. I want to get into your life story because there's so much to cover. Can you just give me an executive summary synopsis of just kind of where you grew up, how you grew up, and then we'll get into some of the other stuff?*

JOE CAPUTO: Yeah, high level, at the end of the day, I think when it's so hard to talk about yourself and like encompass your entire life, I guess. But definitely a lot of different stages. I always tell people, I feel like I've lived many different lives at 36 years old. I grew up in Orange County, but I've lived all throughout California, Southern California, Northern California, pond desert, inland empire, do a lot of traveling, but you know, kind of life stages. I had a really rough childhood in the sense that I made it tough for myself. Come from a divorced family. Mom and stepdad had to work constantly. It was kind of self-governing yourself as a child growing up. I had an older sister, she's passed now, older brother, but you know, they always focused on themselves and they were kids in their own right. I got in trouble a lot growing up, arrested when I was 13, again when I was 16.

I was arrested again when I was 18, overdosed twice when I was 19. That was like stage one of my life. Then really, after overdosing, I'm sure we'll go into these backstories for each one of those four, cause those four are in of itself long stories. From there, you know, I really kind of changed my life and got focused into business and work.

Some of that was still in play when I was using, but certainly not focused on it. I shifted; you move addictions. I always tell people this, if you're an addict, you never stop being an addict. I switched my addiction from crime and drugs and all of that, if you will, to business and just became really hyper-focused on that. Unfortunately, as a result of that, I treated my body really badly.

I gained a lot of weight. I'm a big guy in general, but I went from weighing 300 pounds to up to 400 plus pounds. I think that was my next stage of life where I kind of mastered business to some degree. I was like, okay, I really need to change my lifestyle and focus more on my mental health. I really got into fitness and lost 150 pounds.

That's a whole new stage of life, right? I lost 150 pounds and then kind of rebuilt my body and put on about 30 plus pounds of muscle. Now I weigh like 280 and I've kept that kind of frame. Then that enters into a whole new range of life and really where I'm kind of at now, where my life is focused on first and foremost, taking care of myself and the people who are around me and making sure I have a well-balanced life. I think fitness became that next kind of addiction, and it keeps me very grounded. It's a very good addiction to have, but you still have to kind of maintain it. I go to the gym seven days a week, people like lose their shit when they hear that, but it keeps me grounded and helps me focus on my business and the things that are important to me.

Life has just kind of been balanced out between business, health, wellness, and really the next stage that we'll start to talk about which is exploring the option of creating a life coaching business that will allow me to potentially help other people with these multiple different things that I've struggled with throughout my life.

STREET TALES: *We will get into it, but I just want to, at this point, cause having gotten to know you, I've known you for almost a year, maybe over a year. When I first met you, I remember thinking this dude is huge and I am not a small man either. I know it was one of the first things we talked about, the fitness side of your life and how people will try to minimize the amount of work that goes into attaining peak fitness.*

You're like, yeah, I'm up at three in the morning. Do my walks and then you're very regimented in your fitness. And like you said, people hear, "I work out seven days a week." They're like, "Oh my God, that's too much. He's got a problem." As long as you are smart and take care of your body, it is something that is very attainable. You're getting my mind going now and how fitness and business and success in general takes a mindset and you have to grind.

Some of the most successful people I have ever known are up at 4 a.m. either working or working out or whatever it is, but they're up every day and they tend to be very regimented in how they live their life. They typically are not free wheeling and dealing and trying to figure out shit on the fly. They have a game plan, they stick to it, they grind through the hard parts. It's really interesting because the high-functioning individuals I am referring to typically don't get overly excited about their success because they just assumed they would be successful due to the amount of work they have put into whatever it might be.

JOE CAPUTO: Maria and I were having this conversation on the way here and have this conversation often, but you know, it's very hard for me to be content. One of the problems is, because I'm so regimented, I do accomplish a lot more than probably the average person. Now I don't have any formal business training or education, so I have to be very intentional about what I set out and do. But I've figured out a system. I call it preparation, routine, and follow-through. My three pillars. And I tell people, just think of like to think of a three-legged chair. If any of the legs are missing, then it ceases to be a functional chair. The whole chair becomes useless. For me, it's those three strong pillars and you're all right. I'm very regimented, you know, about what I do. And it does allow me to accomplish a lot of things.

STREET TALES: *Okay, let's dive into growing up and what led to the man you are today.*

The Turn to Criminal Activity at an Early Age

JOE CAPUTO: Yeah, so my family, and I will not point blame at my mom or anybody, but at the end of the day, my mom worked very hard and still works very hard today, but has a very low income and divorced with my dad when I was very young.

Mentally, I became a very hyper-focused and aware of wealth. Kind of selfishly, I wanted to figure out how to get out of poverty. Money was always a focus for me at very young age. I'm the type of kid that legitimately would take the avocadoes from my neighbor's tree and then sell them. I would do car washes, garage sales, whatever it took to put money in my pocket.

The problem is, that when you're a kid and you're 13 years old, you never really make a substantial amount where it makes any difference. I was also an angry kid and it was hard for me to control. I went to therapy and tried all that self-help stuff, but I believe I was just angry my parents were divorced, and ultimately, I just wanted attention.

I started hanging out with a couple different kids in the neighborhood that probably weren't the best kids to be hanging out with. We all had the mindset to just make money, which led to many problems down the road.

I try to tell each story individually and will start when I was 13. My school had a play that they were putting on and they were raising money and doing all this stuff. I was part of the drama class. I noticed that the teacher was putting the money away in a regular cupboard. Real loose, like just a file cabinet, like a little single key lock type of thing. I was always hyper aware of my surroundings and especially when money was being stored or collected.

I told one of my good friends at that time, "Man, they're putting all this money in a cupboard and it could be thousands of dollars. I bet we could come back on the weekend and just take it. Nobody would know because there aren't any cameras and the security is pretty much nonexistent." They didn't have ring or nest cameras back then, so it was pretty wide open. That is literally what I did. Unfortunately, I misused my intelligence for criminal shit. I put some tape on the back door exit so the door wouldn't latch and when Saturday rolled around, I walked right into the classroom and took the money.

I went right to that cabinet, and it didn't take much effort to get the cabinet open. I took all the cash and coins, but I left the checks. I got away with it for a few months and even gave one of my friends who went with me a little money as well. Keep in mind, I was 13 years old, and this was thousands of dollars, but I was smart enough to know how to hide it. I remember I wanted some new shoes and clothes and paid the cashier to call my mom and tell her I won a contest or something so she wouldn't be suspicious of my new things. Real criminal shit even at 13.

I tried to justify it in my mind that at least my mom didn't have to buy me clothes and shoes so I was helping her in that way, very selfish thought process.

I had other friends that were kind of in the same situation I was, so I just gave them money. Then because they were my friends and I was 13 and not as intelligent, I told them what I did. Months went by and people started to put the pieces together. Some of my friends I had given money to were not as smart about how they spent their money or who they talked to. One of the lunch ladies called them into the office, and they broke down right away and just said what happened. So, then they called me in. The police officer there scolded me and my friends who just ratted me out and told them I had all the money.

To make matters worse, I was thinking about being a cop at the same time I was doing all this devious shit. I was in the explorer program and was excited to be a cop when I grew up. That's how the cop got me to break and eventually admit to everything. The cop broke me down, and I had immediate regret for what I had done and how stupid it all was, and I felt like I had just ruined my life.

It's crazy to think about now, being in junior high school thinking and acting the way I was. My son is 15 years old now and I could never imagine getting a call from the school and them telling me my son was arrested for stealing thousands of dollars from the drama program. I would freak out and can't even wrap my head around it.

Me and my buddies were in the cop cars and all my other friends from the explorer program were watching me get arrested. I should have had regret after all of that happened and I finished my community service, but I didn't. The experience pushed me even further and made me even worse.

You know, again, I was really kind of left to my own devices and a couple of years go by and I got into high school and I was one those kids. I smoked and drank very young. My parents would have a lot of parties. We'd have people over. We had a little bar in our living room, literally in our living room. My mom's friends would come over. I'd serve them drinks and charge them money. When high school started, I still had that business mindset. That is how I got arrested when I was 16.

I became part of a party crew. Basically, you would throw parties and charge people to get into them. I had a relationship a liquor store where the guys knew that I was obviously not 21. I'd go in there. I'd buy cases of Mickey's 32 ounce or 40 ounces, he would charge me a $1.50, and I would sell them for five bucks.

STREET TALES: *What age range was this?*

JOE CAPUTO: This was like 15, 16. But this is where it escalated really bad. I would go to parties and sell weed, which was illegal then. When you go to enough of these parties you can easily flip an ounce of weed and I was making real money at that point.

I had a job, I won't say where, let's just say it was very convenient. People would literally drive through, come to me and I would give them their bag. They would give me cash and then they would drive off. Versus all the other kids my age hiding it in their backpack, taking like one little gram to school.

Brass Knuckles and Switch Blades are Felonies in California

JOE CAPUTO: That escalated and that started to build up. Then I went to this party, and these guys caught me selling and they were like, "What are you fucking doing here?" These guys were selling coke. I wasn't into that at that time. They basically applied a lot of pressure on me. I said, "Listen, man, why are you guys giving me shit for selling weed at your party?" "Because we're selling coke and this is the money that we're making." I was like, "Well, wait a minute. I want to do that, want to escalate this." We kind of fell into this arrangement where I started doing that. They were my suppliers and I was selling their stuff. When you get into that world, that's a completely different world. Now I was showing up to parties with coke and selling to people. I never carried a gun or anything of that nature, but I would definitely get into fights with people over dealing. Yeah, different world.

I was a big kid, six foot two, six foot three, kind of in that kind of range at that time. I started buying knives, brass knuckles, switch blades, things of that nature. Again, not really like thinking much of it, two very different worlds. I had all of these in my car and one day I was driving home, and I got pulled over.

The cop said, "Let me see your driver's license." I think I like ran a red light or I was speeding or something. I opened my glove compartment and the car I had at that time was a Nissan Altima. This is also a funny story. I don't want to downplay, but I also don't want to glorify but I was working a day job.

I was making all of this additional money. My mom thought all my money was coming from my day job. I literally bought my car cash. At 16 years old, bought a $30,000 car. I'm sitting in my beautiful little Nissan Altima, which for me was glorious. I opened my glove compartment and in my center console, the car had like two different center consoles. One was just the top where my wallet was but the second inside of it had brass knuckles and something else. I opened the wrong one and I basically flashed it to the cop and I put it back. I kind of looked at him and he looked at me and put his hand on his gun. He said, "Put your hands on the steering wheel." I put my hands on the steering wheel. He said, What's in your center console?" I was like, fuck. "It's brass knuckles." "Why do you have brass knuckles?" he wanted to know.

"I don't know." He ended up opening my center console. They put me in the back of their car. I had brass knuckles, switch blades, knives. I also had a machete and a bat in my trunk. Well, they're all felonies. The switch blade and the brass knuckles are felonies in California.

I was 16 years old. My car was getting towed away. They were calling my parents. This was the second time I'd been arrested. They started grilling me because then they were like, "What the fuck? Why do you have all these weapons? Like what's going on?" I'm like, "I just need to protect myself." My parents call bullshit, and they wanted to know what's going on. My mom pretty much put two and two together, and then she really started freaking out so that one same thing, you know, I was lucky in hindsight, very lucky that I did good in school. I had great grades.

My anger issues had kind of gotten under control. My teachers wrote me letters of recommendations and I had to do community service. But you get used to making that kind of money. I was like, man, I can't get in trouble for this shit again. The cops were drilling me on what was going on.

The math wasn't mathing. You know what I mean? I got used to making that money. Call it entrepreneur mindset, call it stupidity, call it whatever you want. Over the next two years, I built out this kind of theft ring. I switched gears because I wanted to continue making money and came up with this one program with a bunch of my friends who worked at a Target and Walmart, where most teenagers work. This was when CDs were really big, a lot of iPhones and other stuff, iPods, all that stuff were just coming out. Talking to my friends, I figured out a system where I could send somebody in. They would get a cart full of stuff. They would be working during a time that somebody else was working security, and they would walk out and basically have a shopping cart full of stuff. I was the organizer where I would essentially have people make a list of what they wanted and then I would go and sell it to them. At this point, I had also started using drugs. I was smoking weed. I started doing heroin. I started doing crack.

This whole party frame really kind of got me into everything. It was just a bad period in my life. This was stage one of my life where it was like a crash course. I don't know why I chose to do those things. It just somehow started happening. Now all my friends were partyers.

You know, everyone's recreational and I think that should have been my intention, but now I was 17, 18 years old. My parents moved my senior year of high school and that is when it all really kind of came to a boil. That's when I really started using. My parents bought a house in Sun City, which is super far from Orange County. They moved out, and I was able to talk with our landlord because we were renting a house at that period of time.

I got a group of friends together where we literally had a house. I was 17 years old, still finishing high school, graduating high school. I had this house; I had a party crew. had all this loose income. Dude, I would literally go to work from 3pm to 11pm, get off work, party till like three, four in the morning, sleep, check in on my little day business, and then go back to work.

I started using and my friend at that time passed away and that really like drove me over the edge. He was 18. Another best friend of mine passed away when he was 19. I got into anything that would numb my pain. I was not thinking clearly. I had this stupid business that's not really a business, right? But it was helping me financially. One day, the people who were supposed to go and do it were like, "Hey, I can't go."

Well, I had a routine set up, right? I went to go do it myself. Turns out it was a whole setup. They had finally figured everything out. The security person that was supposed to be working that day wasn't working that day. But they were texting from his phone. I went myself, I put all the stuff together, went to go walk out and like six security guards basically jumped me and the police were already there.

It was probably the best thing that ever happened to me. I was now 18. Now it was real. Not like when I was 13, when I was 16, and was slapped on the wrist, having teachers write stuff. This was what you want for your life? I got into a fight and actually also what saved me. The security guards grabbed me and I put up a fight. It was five on one and it turned into a full-on fight. They ended up breaking my big toe or not breaking it, but they like stomped it out and it completely ballooned up. That was all on camera. I went to jail, big boy jail. Went to county, was there for three days. I was super embarrassed. I didn't want to call anybody. They towed my truck. By this time, I had also gotten rid of my Altima. I got a freaking Nissan Titan at 18 years old. It was just like everything was exploding.

Here I was, sitting there for three days in jail looking around like *is this who I'm going to be?* You know what mean? I know people will sometimes say the system doesn't work, but to me, the system fucking worked. I was sitting there for the third time being arrested. I was scared. I'm a big dude, but I was fucking scared. You know, stripped down, butt naked.

Blacks all go to the left, Mexicans to the right, white people straight forward, dudes asking me about my tattoos. My friend had passed away; He was born in 1988. They're like, "What does the 88 means?" Trying to immediately put me with all the skinheads, I'm not kidding.

I didn't want to shower during those three days. I was thinking *I'm going to get raped in there.* It scared me enough to where I was like, *dude, is this my fucking life?*

I didn't call anybody, didn't make any phone calls from there other than to my family, I disappeared. I was supposed to go to work. I didn't show up to work. My boss, that was not like me, so he called my mom and my emergency contacts. Obviously, he figured out what was going on. Monday rolled around and my mom and my grandma had already posted bail and it was just embarrassing. I had done all of this because I wanted money. I had enough cash to pay for a good lawyer. I paid my grandma back for posting my bail, and I got a good lawyer because I knew I was in some fucking trouble. Luckily, they didn't have enough proof that it was conspiracy and a grand theft criminal organization. That would be some big boy charges.

It was another felony.

STREET TALES: *I understand what you're saying about money and knowing what it's like to be hungry, to not have what you see your other classmates, or your friends have and you're just like,* why can't I have that? *I think for me, because what you're talking about, I knew kids like that in high school. Everybody kind of knows the deal and what kind of adds up and what doesn't.*

I was always on the outside, and I knew what was going on. I always say it was my grandma and my grandfather praying over me, and you know, they would always call and check up on me and sports also helped me because I very easily could have slipped into that as well. I have many friends that I graduated high school with and a lot of them are dead now from either overdosing or in prison. One of my closest friends, again, he was very similar to what you're talking about with the thefts in the circles and stuff. He was like, "I was go-

ing to college. I'm going to Miami to sell coke." And I said, "That's a terrible idea. Please don't do that." It didn't work out well for him. I understand what you're saying. That feeling of wanting to be self-sufficient and you don't have the resources. The easiest way to do it sometimes is the criminal route.

JOE CAPUTO: I'm very humble about my life, and I'm very appreciative of the struggles and challenges and think they made me who I am, but at the end of the day, like when you're in that mindset, you know, you're doing wrong, but somehow you just do it anyway. It's embarrassing, and it is tough to have those conversations. Even now, as a business professional, if somebody asked me about it, I'm not shy to let them know that I used to be an addict and I'm recovered.

I'm not shy to let them know that I've done harm. But when you start talking about a criminal path, it follows you forever. Know what I mean? The reality is, yeah, based on the criminal system, it fucking could. When you fill out a resume and it asks you those questions and all this stuff, that was one of the things that I thought about a lot. Those three days, man, it gives you a lot to think about.

I like to self-evaluate. I have good emotional intelligence too. I could figure out the room and what's going on. Coming out of that, luckily, with the timing of everything, I feel like is very important because what ended up happening was, I literally got out, paid my court fees, did all of that. Lawyers started doing what they needed to do. Mind you again, through this whole time, I had a day job.

I had a good job and my bosses and everybody cared enough about me to care if I was okay. I didn't tell them all the details, obviously, but they also didn't care. They were just like, "What are you going to do?" Well, I was also very good at what I did from a day job perspective.

While I was fighting my court case, there was this opportunity for me to move up north and a salary job opportunity at 18 years old.

I was like, okay, I've got a road to my left and a road to my right. If I stay here, I've got this party house. I have this whole persona that I've created for myself over the years. Now, mind you, nobody really gives a shit about that anymore. Right? All my friends, they know how I was during that period of time when people who I've known for my whole life, were saying, "You're totally different person." I'm just a completely different person and I love that.

Navigating the Right Path & My First Overdose

JOE CAPUTO: I looked at these roads and I was like, man, *I'm going to go to the right.* I applied for that job opportunity. I got awarded it even with the mistakes I had made. I packed my fucking bags and I moved to Northern California. I fought my case and got it dropped down significantly to a misdemeanor and something that I was eligible after five years to get removed from my record, which I did, absolutely. But when I was living in Northern California, I literally had to come back every other weekend because I had community service. I had to drive back. That was also a struggle. I was starting a new job or new position, and it was a leadership position. I have extra money, not the money I was making before, but a real job. You know what mean? Real good money, consistent salary every two weeks, that check comes in. It was the same check.

My friend had passed away, and I had all these traumas that my mom did her best to try to get me into counseling so I could deal with those things. But I just couldn't deal with the pain of losing one of my friends so young. I would do all kinds of different drugs and try to disappear. It came to a head because when I moved, I was about 18 and a half.

For about six months, I was heavy drug user. On my 19th birthday, I came back to Orange County. I'd already finished my program, finished everything, and I was done. I came back to celebrate my birthday and we all started smoking. Then all of sudden we started doing lines. Then all of a sudden, something happened.

I have no idea. I don't remember, couldn't tell you. I could have killed someone during that period. I have no idea what happened, but I know that I woke up in a hotel room that, apparently, I had rented. I was throwing up on myself. Basically, I woke up choking on my own vomit and I turned off to the side, spit up whatever and I was butt naked. I'd pissed and shit myself.

That was my first overdose. Wow. I thought to myself, *man, fuck dude, what am I doing? I was trying to get away from all this.* You know what I mean? *What am I fucking doing here?* I got my shit together, went back up North. By this time, I had gotten another job promotion and moved even further up North. I'm having the successful career during the day. But when I was by myself, I was just doing all kinds of stupid shit.

I was trying to party and do all this. I was like, *all right, I'm not doing that again.* Cause that type of overdose isn't really like an overdose, right? I mean, it was bad. Don't get me wrong, pissing and shitting themselves, most people won't admit to that, but I basically vomited and woke myself up. Had I not been more so on my side, I could have drowned in my own throw up, could have been that typical kind of overdose, right? When I went home and I was like, *I'm not going to do it anymore. I'm just not.*

STREET TALES: *I've seen that.*

JOE CAPUTO: One week went by and I was good. I was like, fuck yeah, dude. I'm so good. I'm doing all right. Then two weeks went by and then, that itch just kicks in and I was like, fuck it. I can go to a party and just drink. It's not a big deal. I went to this next party and the same thing, man. This up north. One thing leads to another and same thing. We started smoking, started doing lines, started doing heroin and coke.

I've told this story before on my podcast too, about the second overdose. What ended up happening was, I wasn't done, and I was just chasing it, dude. I was trying to kill myself because, for whatever reason, I don't know, I just couldn't deal with the pain, you know? There was not really much pain for me, but I didn't feel like I was doing much with my life.

Experiencing Loss, My Second Overdose, & Betrayal

JOE CAPUTO: You know what I mean? I had a friend pass away when he was 18, a friend passed away when I was 19 or when he was 19. One was in a motorcycle crash. He didn't have his license. I got him a job with me. He bought a motorcycle. There's some self-guilt there. He didn't get his permit. He was riding his motorcycle and cop tried to pull him over. He took off. He we didn't have his helmet on all the way or buckled and a truck saw that police were chasing him. They pulled in front of him, slammed on the brakes. He hit the back of the truck, went into a coma for four days and passed away. That's right. The other one went to a party, left the party, and fell asleep while he was driving home, and crashed this car.

STREET TALES: *I have had similar instances throughout my life and unfortunately have had several friends die from reckless behav-*

ior. I had kids very young, and I believe that kept me from being as reckless with my life as some of my friends. The stories you're telling could have easily been my own story. Thank God I had something to ground me and keep me from making potentially deadly decisions.

JOE CAPUTO: I think this is why I just kept chasing because I didn't really have something to ground me quite yet. For that second overdose, and this is where it all kind of comes together, because my friends do play a crucial part in that, right? From a pain perspective, I was trying to get rid of that pain, but also from a survival perspective, it's really what changed my life and got rid of this whole stage of theft and crime and bullshit. My friends were all done partying, but I wasn't. I attempted to cook my own crack. I thought the smartest idea was to take the coke that we had, obviously you kind of know somewhat how to do it. I'm sure some people have no idea how to it, but if you're in that business or around that industry, you kind of figure it out. I didn't have baking soda, but I did have Ajax.

I was so fucked up that I decided to use Ajax and I made this big blue crystal. I was like, *oh, it fucking worked. That's wild.* I smoked it and you know, immediately like a television tuning out, like an old school television, when just the outside turns black, that happened. That's what I remember before everything shut down.

I don't know if my heart stopped. I don't know if I just got super high and just passed out. I have no idea. Ultimately, to the people that were there, I died and they freaked out. They took my body and they dragged me down these stairs into their little carport. It was basically like a garage slash carport, and they dropped my body there, went back upstairs, and they were freaking out. Two of the guys were talking about what to do with my body. In this process, I wake up. Just like the television went off, all of sudden, the first thing is I started hearing stuff and it's painful, almost like a loud, sharp pain in my ears. I started hearing like echoing, double echoing. Then I felt pain in my chest. Jesus, bro. I don't know if I had a heart attack or what happened, but I felt a lot of pain in my chest.

I remember grabbing my chest. It was pitch black. I couldn't really see much, but then I just started hearing my two friends talking about what to do with my body. There was a third friend just crying his eyes out. It was kind of like a college community and there were a bunch of these marshes, like a swampy kind of area that they could literally dispose of me in if they wanted to. Do I think they actually were going to do that? No, I don't think they were. They were just so scared that they were just trying to figure out how to get out of the situation. They talked about maybe throwing me in the marshes. They talked about cutting me up. my God, bro. You're listening to this? I was trying to gather my strength up. Then they made the more logical decision. "We should just drive him back to his apartment and leave some of the drugs there."

STREET TALES: *At any point did somebody think they should take you to a hospital?*

JOE CAPUTO: No, no, never. Not one time, dude. Not fucking one time. "We should put him in the car, get him to his house, throw him in his bed, leave the drugs. Somebody will find him." Now, the guy who was crying was like my roommate, so he would have had to been the one to call the cops. They should have known that all wouldn't have worked out anyway. But I woke up, and now I was just fucking mad.

I went up the stairs and got into a fight with these guys, destroyed their apartment, got my friend and we went home.

STREET TALES: *I think that's a justified response, bro. The story you're telling me is wild. That's fucked. I don't know what I would do if I heard my friends talking about my body like that.*

JOE CAPUTO: Well, again, this is where I feel like my whole life really changed because then I got home and...

STREET TALES: *Hold on, let me ask you, I never asked you this. At any point, did you go to the hospital? On either one?*

JOE CAPUTO: No. I went home, I went into my room, and I had a calendar and I went to the date. I'm like, *I'm fucking done. Like a second overdose. I'm fucking done.* It was October 14. I circled the date, the 14th. That's actually when my first friend passed away. Now the crazy math on this, the dates aligned by 14 months. My first friend passed away on the 14th and 14 months later my other friend and then it would have been me. The way the things work out. For the next three days, I went through full detox. It was rough, you know what I mean?

STREET TALES: *Can you explain that just a little bit because I've only heard how rough it is.*

JOE CAPUTO: Well, the problem is I was doing so many different things that I was experiencing different highs and lows. I would smoke a lot. I would smoke my heroin for the most part. I did inject many times, but I was more of a smoker. Really, it was just a lot of headaches, lot of vomiting, your stomach, your intestines, you don't want to eat, but then you're getting stomach cramps, and it was just very painful sweating my ass off.

It was just really painful.

STREET TALES: *Had you steeled your mind that this is going to suck? Did you know this was coming?*

JOE CAPUTO: I knew that that would just happen in general because the previous two weeks weren't that bad because I continued to smoke and stuff like that, so my original mindset was, I'm just going to stop doing anything aside from drink and smoke. Okay, that was my original mindset. I thought if I smoked, it would get my mind off of stuff. I thought, if *I smoke weed, it's not a big deal.* I decided I was done with everything. I never stopped drinking. I think, you know, that's something I've explored over the years, but it's not really a crutch for me.

I'm not an alcoholic or anything. I did occasionally drink. Regardless, it was the best thing that could have ever happened to me because once I got through that, all the people that wanted to hang out with me disappeared. The whole experience is what saved me.

I started thinking, *what a fucking piece of shit friend you are. These are two dudes that you grew up with had no choice in their loss of life. You're poisoning your body literally.* I went to their funerals, saw what their parents went through. My mom would have experienced that. You know what mean? Yeah, all the shit I put her through.

Her working her ass off for fucking 20 bucks an hour or whatever the fuck she was making. It gave me such perspective, and I just kept thinking about their parents and thinking about them in their coffins and thinking about how they had no choice.

STREET TALES: *My friend, Dave Tarbox, talks about that as well. The impact when it finally hits you at a very young age. For you though, you had this other successful side. You knew you could do it.*

JOE CAPUTO: My daughter just turned 20 yesterday, and when we had dinner, she was telling me she just realized she is the same age that I was when I had her. I told her that it was scary. I didn't know shit and was trying to deal with my own stuff and be a father.

I also look at my son. He's 15. I can't even imagine two years ago getting a call that he was arrested or like a year from now he's getting arrested again. That's why I had to develop emotional intelligence. I'm hyper aware of other people, and I can put myself in my mom's shoes now. It must have been so hard for her dealing with all the shit she was dealing with and all the other stresses that life brings you in general and then having to deal with me.

I'm my mom's youngest. Just the fear of, what's going to happen to my kid?

STREET TALES: *It's odd because you have two kids, I have two kids, and very similar-ish backgrounds, obviously, not quite to the extent that you're talking about, but you think about that from a parent's perspective, and imagine your son was dealing with this, and you didn't have any idea, or you couldn't see it, and then you realize, holy fuck, the way it would make me feel as a parent. I don't wish what you're talking about on anyone.*

JOE CAPUTO: I don't wish for people to gain experience this way, but it does make you much more aware of what's going on and how to read people.

There's a funny song that I like listening to and it says that hundred bad days leads to a hundred interesting stories at the end of the day. Am I happy that I went through all of that? Now I am, absolutely. Because I feel like it gives me a completely different perspective that most people don't have. If I would have stopped there, literally overdosed and died, that would be the memory that everybody has of me, this fucking delinquent.

That is a motivator for me, which enters the next chapter, right? I know because I survived through that. I overcame that. It gives me a lot of motivation to move forward. It also humbles me because when I see other people who are not in a good position, I never look at them and think, well, that is exactly who that person is. That person is a piece of shit. I think, well, that person might be in that position right now. That guy or girl in five years from now can be a completely different person. I never judge people based on their current situation.

STREET TALES: *I had to learn that. I really didn't learn that until I became a cop in Florida. I grew up knowing about that but not in it. Then, my world was college and sports and then banking and all that. Then I became a cop and I found myself after a couple of years having conversations with prostitutes, homeless people, stuff like that.*

You learn that just because of their situation, it doesn't make them a bad person or a piece of shit, right? You start to learn about what's going on and how it impacted them. I have a lot of respect for you and other men in my life that have gone through similar instances and are willing to talk about it. They're willing to talk about their experiences, not to glorify their behavior, but to explain what happened and what they learned from it.

Acknowledge that it was embarrassing, and it doesn't define you, right? I have friends of mine who have similar instances and all they want to do is put it in a black box and never want anybody to ever know. I say that it will come out eventually. People know. I'm not telling anyone how to live their life, but I have nothing but respect.

We All Wear Masks or Put on a Façade

STREET TALES: *On this podcast, I have a lot of people talking about mental health and dealing with these traumas. I'm sure you know, there's a lot of men, not just in law enforcement, military, but in a lot of professional careers, who don't want anyone to know about anything they're dealing with. They're like voodoo, witchcraft, mind magic. I say, "Bro, you're dealing with a lot of shit. It could help you."*

JOE CAPUTO: I think, ultimately, we like to put on facades. Everyone you meet has layers. I said when someone meets me today, their perception of me is based off of who I am, how I present myself, what I'm doing, whether it's business or health or wellness, whatever it is, that's their perception.

As they get comfortable, and then as they find out about these other layers, they're sometimes more impressed or they start opening up and sharing their own experiences. Every single person has these layers. So many people, like you said, that just box things up and put it aside. Like it never happened. That's not how you get through things. It's okay, because guess what? Everyone you talk to has a story.

It doesn't matter what's in their bank account. It doesn't matter what their job title is. It doesn't matter what they're wearing on their back or what car they're driving. Every single person has a story and how they've gotten here, what they're dealing with. Everyone has something they're dealing with. Everyone has good people in their life. Everyone has bad people in their life.

STREET TALES: *I've talked to my kids, and I always hold myself to a standard that when they turn 30, I'll know if I did a good job or not. I never wanted them to hold me on a pedestal. I've told them about the mistakes. I've told them, probably when they were too young, I fucked up a lot.*

I've learned a lot of fucking lessons the hardest way possible you could ever learn them. I don't want you to do that. I will say for the most part, they get it. I think my son wants to learn his lessons the hard way too. But my baby, she's like, "Hearing you and watching my brother, I think I'm going to go this path." I mean, everyone's got their own path to walk.

JOE CAPUTO: I think with older siblings too. There is that difference where you can learn from them. My brother, as soon as he turned 17 and a half, had my mom sign the papers. He went into the army. He never came back. He's 39 now and he never came back. He's always been in the military. He got focused and took off and created his own life and never looked back. My sister did her best, but she was always just kind of in and out of things. She went through a snit of drug addiction as well and, unfortunately, developed a heart issue and passed away when she was 41 years old. I look around at families and one person could be a doctor or a lawyer and the next person could be a homeless man on the corner. Two people, two decisions. I had two roads in front of me. I made a decision. I decided I was going to go the other route. I've been through a lot. There's no coming back. It's just a decision. Everything in your life is just making the right choice.

STREET TALES: *I'm the oldest and I have younger siblings, my sister and my brother. I think about those things too. What were your thoughts on your brother when he left? Did you feel like he left you, abandoned you? Are you proud? What does that look like?*

JOE CAPUTO: I'm proud of him now. I totally understood why he left. I think he did the right thing. I know we were not close growing up. We're only two years apart and usually kids that are that age would be very close, but what happened I think was that I stole a lot of attention.

My brother was a middle child. My sister was always fucking something up, and then I was always fucking something up. My brother was just like, *what the fuck?* Unfortunately, he didn't have the childhood that he probably deserved because he was just stuck in the middle. He wasn't a mentor for me. He didn't do any of that. I don't fault him for that. He just focused on himself. He did what he needed to do and he made the right choice for himself. I don't fault him for that.

STREET TALES: *I was the oldest. At 18, I kind of did the same thing. I did what I thought was best for me, and I never really looked back. Now, 23 years later, I feel guilty because I basically left my sister and that's when she started going a little off the rails and I wasn't there. I don't want to say I didn't care, like I wasn't like checking in. I was focused on my own shit.*

Then my brother's eight years younger than me. There was a vast gap. Most of his childhood I was in high school, college, and then I had a wife. I had two kids. My whole life was completely different than middle school, so there was a vast disconnect, and we've connected now in adulthood, but I'm dealing with a little bit of guilt on that.

JOE CAPUTO: Well, there's nothing for you to be guilty about because ultimately you could also play the story back, and you could have been there for your sister to give her advice and then she would make the same choice. People make their own choices at the end of the day. What I've noticed about people who are not in the same positions as people who they want to be a lot of times it's because they're playing the victim mentality. Regardless, they would have made their own choices. But let's move on. The second overdose happens; you go through the withdrawals and now we're talking about the rehabilitation. Looking at you now, knowing you now, it's fucking wild. When you first started telling me about it, I would never have assumed. I figured you were just a fucking rockstar from day one.

I think it's a facade thing, right? While you're at work and you're getting the day job done, then you go home and nobody's there and you're doing all this other shit, nobody knows, right? I was living a little bit of my life in a facade during that period. I carried that over to the next. I wanted to be successful. I've always wanted to be successful from a young age.

Business, I was clearly good at it. I was literally selling avocados I stole from my neighbor, or having garage sales, I was always creating these little money-making schemes. While they were wrong, the enterprises generated enough income for me to do all this other stuff. I realized there had to be a company that would hire me to do something.

I wanted a good enough job to give me opportunities and the ability to make money instead of fucking around doing all this illegitimate stuff, trying to get money too fast. It was a perfect time.

From a Life of Crime to a Life of Business!

STREET TALES: *How did you change your focus from illegitimate stuff to more business-minded endeavors?*

JOE CAPUTO: I took a few business classes, and I got really into Franklin Covey and Stephen Covey. It's basically crash courses on business. This guy created the four disciplines of execution and goal setting. I started reading books like a book called *Good to Great*. I read about emotional intelligence. I was all in. I didn't have money to go to college. I didn't want to take on debt.

I just wanted to learn, got into David Ramsey, *Rich Dad, Poor Dad*, and just started understanding all of that. This company just kept growing and I kept advancing with them. I moved to Northern California, to Santa Clara. Then I moved to Palm Desert. Then I actually got a promotion and moved back to the location that I started at. I literally was running this. I made it into a half a million-dollar business at 21 years old.

I was running a half a million-dollar business for this company. They were cool and they did this employee stock share program where literally you could take your quarterly bonuses and get shares in the company instead for up to half of it. I did that every single time. When the company finally sold, I got my first actual company ownership dividend, and I went and bought a house.

STREET TALES: *Did you have like a mentor or was it just you consuming knowledge?*

JOE CAPUTO: I definitely have had mentors over the years. I had a business mentor that really kept me in line. My boss at that time, he's my son's godfather. He owns his own company now. During that period of time, he was my business mentor but only for the job. He wanted to make sure I was getting the job done. I would see successful people getting into fitness around that time too.

I would look at people and I'd go, *that person's in a better situation than I am, or I want to be like that person. I'm going to go ask them how they did it. I'm just going to absorb whatever I can.* You also have to re- member I had all this extra time. I wasn't partying anymore. I thought, *what am I going to do with this time?* I'm an addict, right? So, I need to keep myself busy. What can I do? Books and that type of experience.

I found out that every city has this thing called Small Business Devel- opment Centers. Their whole focus and their whole job are to take a person, show them how to build a business, open it, and help you get funding. I literally pretended I was going to open a business, went through a six-month course on how to grow a business just so I could learn how to do it. Excel and accounting and all of that.

I'm running this half a million-dollar business for somebody else. I get my first dividend and then I get a house. Well, at that time, the stock market had crashed. The housing market had crashed. I bought my 3,200 square foot house for $216,000. It had been built in 2007. I bought it in 2012. I learned at that period of time how to leverage home equity. When the market corrected, I learned that I could bor- row against the equity, and I could have more money and then I could go and do stuff with that. That was like the smallest little taste of the pie. It was like a $35,000 check or something.

I was clearly successful at what I did, but they were trapping me be- cause of my age. I wanted to do more. I was so hungry and they wanted me to calm down. "This isn't like a rodeo cowboy." There was another company in LA, and they were super focused on growth. They were like, "Listen, if you want take a step back and join our company, we'll let you advance as fast as you want to." I had two roads, and I thought, well, I know where road one leads.

I've learned a lot from them, but they've taught me what they've taught me. It's time to go to my next opportunity. I joined that company in LA and they didn't know shit. All the stuff that I had learned, I started applying there and literally within 30 days, I found out that they were missing about a million dollars of revenue and they had no idea.

They wanted to know, "How did you figure this out?" I ran them through the process, and I told them, you have to do this. You have to track everything like that. They were missing a million dollars in billables. My boss at that time asked, "Do you want to take charge of this?" "Yeah, sure, yes, I do." He said, "I can't give you a promotion." I said, "That's fine. Let me fix this problem. When I fix it, we'll have the extra money. You can give me a promotion then." I went and fixed it and he gave me a promotion.

Then he came to me and asked, "Hey, you want to open this new account and every new account you open, I'll give you a percentage so you can make more." Good. From 2013 to 2019, I opened over 60 properties. But I was still working for somebody else. During that period of time, I started to understand how business grew, but I needed to learn culture, needed to learn how to maintain all that.

Now, I was commuting to LA, which is at a minimum an hour and a half each way. I was working 10 to 12 hours a day. Plus, the drive, making it 15, 16-hour days every day, Monday through Friday, sometimes even on a Saturday or Sunday. I really sacrificed about six years of my life to just learn, grow, and create a name for myself.

I was building this business and leveraging the industry that I knew how to do. I took the home equity and started investing in other businesses. I had a friend that wanted to open a cannabis company.

I helped him do that. Grew it, took my portion out, sold my portion off, doubled my money, paid off the home equity. Found the next business that I wanted to invest in. Did that, grew it, sold it, put the money back. I just kept repeating that process.

Changing My Life and My Body!

STREET TALES: *You also own or owned your own companies, correct?*

JOE CAPUTO: Yes, I opened my own consulting company, started having people hire me to come in and do exactly what I did for the first company. I would tell them, "I could find you money. How about this? You don't have to pay me a cent, but for everything I find, I want a percent of it. If I grow your business, you start making hundred thousand dollars more, I want 50% of that or 25% or whatever the share was.

I still do that today. I'll find small businesses or moderate-sized businesses, and I'll basically go into them and do that. During that six-year period of time though, I was working 16 hours a day, which just abused the fuck out of me.

I beat the shit out of my body, ended up gaining like 100 pounds. I was 400 pounds. I would literally not eat all day, then before I drive home, I would stop at fucking Jack in the Box and order four tacos, a jumbo jack meal with curly fries, a large Coke, which is like 4,000 calories in like one sitting. I ate in my car on the drive.

I went for a standard doctor's checkup and they told me I was diabetic. I needed to be on these cholesterol pills for rest of my life. My sister had already had her heart issues. My brother got diagnosed with blood clotting in his legs that was actually genetic. My grandma passed away from blood clotting in her neck and my dad had just had a heart issue. At this point, I'm like 26. I realize need to change my fucking life. *What am I doing? I've created all this. I have all this knowledge, right? I have all this experience. I have money and I'm just going to be some fat dude that dies. I can't keep up with my kids. What the fuck am I doing?* I drew a line in the sand. I needed to make health a priority. I met this guy who was roughly 26.

I was looking at doing the stomach surgeries and all that stuff, but I literally ran into him at a Denny's bathroom. I said, "Hey, man, like you've lost like fucking 150, 200 pounds, right? Did you do surgery? He's said, "No, I watched this documentary called *Fat, Sick, and Nearly Dead* and it changed my life." "Fuck, what is it about?" It's about a business guy who does a 60-day juice fast and loses like 80 pounds. He was taking all these pills and had all these body rashes. He completely cured himself. There's another guy in that same documentary that lost like a hundred plus pounds. He was a truck driver. I thought, *if these motherfuckers can do this. I can do it. Right?* Yeah. Sure enough, I decided to do a juice cleanse. I set out to just do a three day. I was like, no way I'm doing 60 days, let me just do three days. When you get through three days, your body just dumps stuff. On day three, I was like, *know what? I can actually do a week.* Then I did seven days and then I was like, *you know what? I can push it a little bit more.* I ended up doing 10 days and then I weighed in. I had lost the 30 pounds in 10 days.

I didn't look amazing. I was still 360 plus pounds, you know, but I was feeling better. In watching that documentary, learned that this is called micronutrients. I decided to dive deeper into this. I ended up signing up to do a nutritionist class, personal trainer class, strength and training, and learned about micronutrients, macronutrients, weight training.

I decided to start doing paleo. Paleo is basically if you hunt it, forage it, if you're a caveman and there's no grocery stores, what would you eat? I basically would do one day paleo, one day juice, one day paleo, one day juice. I did that for a fucking year. Yeah. I lost a hundred pounds literally in that full year. Now I was 300 pounds. Then I started getting into running, and yeah, I can run.

I would run on the treadmill and look at the time and then say, tomorrow I want 15 seconds better. Again, I have an addict mind. When I set my sights on something, I'm going to figure it out. It's just how I'm built. People respect people who are fit.

STREET TALES: *Yes, they do.*

JOE CAPUTO: I lost a hundred pounds. That was a whole conversation. People would see what I was doing. People would see what I was eating and was posting about it. People started to respect that process. Two years in, I lost another 50 pounds. I was down to 250 pounds, but I was basically a runner. I had a runner's body. I was eating like rabbit food. Fuck that. I was big my whole life, especially towards high school all my friends knew me as a big guy. It was kind of scary for some people. Then the other side kicked in where weight training and strength and conditioning took place. I started really understanding that so I ended up putting on about 30 pounds of muscle getting to 280 pounds.

This helped me in business because people respect people who lose weight, who transform their lives. People who have routines and are regimented and disciplined, right? People respect that. I'm a big guy. When I walk in a room, it demands a little bit of attention.

Look good in suits, baby.

STREET TALES: *Not that you could do anything about it either. Even if you didn't want to, it doesn't matter.*

JOE CAPUTO: I sometimes don't notice it. Maria will literally be like, "Do you see all these fucking people look at you?" It was kind of that next ceiling I needed in my life because it got me to a stage where fitness was the therapy I really needed. Where I could take out my anger issues, could bounce myself out. It's self-respect.

You get out what you put in. It's a de-stressor. If work or business, or personal things aren't going right, it's the balance. It was the foundation that I was missing. Today, I moved on from that other company. I built it up as big as I could, learned what I could there. Another company approached me and said, "Hey, listen, we're looking for subject experts. We'll give you partnership shares."

I continued to do my consulting and build other businesses. Then my fitness was in line. I have a regimented mentality and I've got a loving caring partner that supports it and works out probably 10 times harder than me. I feel like I'm entering into that third next life stage, right?

STREET TALES: *With that being said, what do you have planned for the future?*

JOE CAPUTO: Knowledge is the one thing that has helped me and been able to teach me a lot to then ground myself. I feel like the most respectful thing to do would be to pass that on. I think I need to write a book and come up with a good format where people can digest those learning lessons and experiences from my years that preparation routine follows through a kind of process. I want to do that because I could pass that on. Not from a business perspective, even though doesn't make a dollar, I just want to be able to pass that knowledge on if somebody wants to pick it up and learn. People are always asking me for advice. I love sharing, and I love doing that, but it's challenging to do that if you have a lot of other things going on and you want to be respectful to yourself and to others.

I'm looking at building a life coaching site that people can subscribe to. As part of that, there would be different levels where they'll be able to get some one-on-one coaching so I can help find where they're at and help them get to where they want to go. I feel because of my experiences throughout my life with addiction, with fitness, with business, I could help balance them out wherever they're at.

Also put them in some group classes so they can gain some knowledge and experience from other people who are going through different things, bring some people together. I really think that's the next stage for me in continuing what I do. I love the business industry that I'm in. I love all the businesses I'm a partner in or an investor in and just to kind of just continue living life, man.

STREET TALES: *I've seen you and worked out with you, and it blows my mind because you're a big dude. You're grinding, but whatever it is, or you put off, people come up to you and start tapping you. "Hey, can I ask you a question?" You're always very generous. You always give that time. Whether you wanted to or not, I think it was inevitable for you.*

My only other thing was that you need to restart that podcast, brother, because again, not just your stories, but the advice you give. I know it's hard, especially if you're just going to be talking by yourself. I've done a couple and it feels awkward and weird, but, brother, your experience, your life, and how you keep grinding in your mindset. I have nothing but respect for you, your openness, but also your grind and your drive. The college thing doesn't fucking matter, bro.

I went to business school for those who are wondering, and I've learned more talking to Joe over the last year, and I don't even think they fucking taught me because the books don't teach you how to do it in practice, in real life. Anything you want to leave with?

JOE CAPUTO: You are always going be faced with two roads and it's your decision to make. For those of you that might not feel like you're in the best position right now, all you have to do is make a decision and get out of it. One of my favorite quotes sums this up best:

Two roads diverged in a wood, and I—
I took the one less traveled by,
And that has made all the difference.
—Robert Frost

Story Wrap Up

Joe Caputo has a big personality, and it is clear to anyone who meets him that he is serious about his health, fitness, and appearance. Joe grew up in a less-than-ideal setting, and was drawn to the criminal life at an early age to obtain the life he wanted and felt he deserved. These decisions eventually led to not one but two overdoses and only by the grace of God did he overcome those experiences.

Once again, Joe did not allow a victim mindset to define the rest of his life and has completely overhauled the trajectory of his entire life. Joe is a highly successful business man, is in the best shape of his life, and focuses his energy on his family, his work, and himself. Sometimes extreme addictions can be transferred to promote health and success instead of devastation and death.

Click or scan the QR Code
to hear the podcast interview

with **Bjar Atkins**

The Story of
BJAR ATKINS

I met Bjar "Bj" Atkins at the Hillsborough County Sheriff's Office (HCSO) police academy in 2011. Bj was a former college football player and is hands down one of the strongest men I have ever met in my entire life. His work ethic is second to none. We actually started our law enforcement careers at the HCSO training facility. To paint the picture, the entire recruiting class met in the parking lot of the training facility with freshly shaved heads, jeans, white T-shirts, and tennis shoes and were greeted by a cadre of HCSO training heavies. There was a lot of yelling and sweating and this went on for the next two weeks.

Back then, HCSO maintained a paramilitary training program to speed the change from civilian to law enforcement professional. It was a two-week program, filled with waking up a 4 a.m., sleeping in twin-size bunk beds, lots of running, and making sugar cookies in the sandbox when the class did something wrong or just because we needed it. We would march, fight, shoot, and did I mention the running? There was so much running. I have never been a runner and this 6' 4" 300lb frame was not designed to run miles a day, every day, for extended periods of time lol! Bj and I were in this recruiting class, but I was in such a daze and so tired that I don't think I even registered who everyone was until we got through the first two weeks and made it to the classroom.

For those who don't know, the police academy program is approximately six months long and is filled with legal procedures, constitutional rights, federal laws, state laws, how to conduct investigations, using the tools of the law enforcement trade, so to speak. Every law enforcement professional who carries a Taser or pepper spray must first have those tools used on them. Yes, I have been tazed many times and pepper sprayed even more. I prefer the taser to pepper spray as my reaction to pepper spray is brutal and everyone laughs every single time. You learn very quickly that just because something is non-lethal, it doesn't mean it doesn't hurt more than anything you can possibly imagine.

Bj and I hit it off pretty much day one as we were two of the biggest guys in the class and of course the instructors had to point that out each and every day. We motivated each other when needed and made the training environment as fun as we could and thus began a lifelong friendship that continues to this day.

It's hard to articulate the bonds that are made with your brothers and sisters in law enforcement. I have played sports my entire life and have made good friends along the way. Law enforcement is a different world all together. You have each other's back in some of the most dangerous situations you have ever been in, your background depending of course. You experience heartache, tragedy on an indiscernible level, but also triumphs and heroic moments. People have to understand that law enforcement officers don't just conduct traffic stops and work traffic crashes. Both of which are some of the most dangerous aspects of law enforcement.

We also work child deaths, shootings, sexual assaults, domestic violence, mass shootings, suicides at an unbelievable scale. Each and every day that you put on the police uniform you have no idea what that day will involve. Will you have a slow night and be able to talk to your close friends and law enforcement family? Will you help someone give birth on the side of the road? Or will it be something horrific and dangerous? Bj and I worked all of these types of calls together and had each other's backs for better or worse.

One of our mentors at the sheriff's office explained that law enforcement is a profession instead of a job. Law enforcement professionals have the unique ability to take peoples freedoms away and should not be taken lightly. In order to be a law enforcement professional, you should always be learning, studying, growing, and doing your best to become an expert in your profession. We took that advice and decided together to obtain a master's in criminal justice administration.

While working towards our master's degree, we developed a multi-agency group working with Florida State Probation to monitor recidivist on probation for tier 1 crimes. I am proud to say that even though I left the Hillsborough County Sheriff's Office, the program is still on-going to this day. Most criminals believe that any law enforcement professional that comes into contact with them will automatically know everything about them. Sadly, this is not true and there are many reasons for this, but the idea that all law enforcement agencies in the United States or even within a state communicate with each other is not true. By working in tandem with other agencies, the street cop can bridge the gap with intel and experience. The probation working group works to share information across multiple agencies and focuses on the individuals who contribute to the majority of the crime in a given area.

Bjar Atkins is now a Master Deputy, Traffic Investigator, and a Bomb Technician.

Below is a conversation with Bj and I talking about his life and how we met:

NAVIGATING LAW ENFORCEMENT:
Personal Stories from BJ

STREET TALES: *I've got my boy, my best friend, my brother-in-arms, BJ Atkins on the line. We're going to get into it, a little bit of his life, sports, growing up where he grew up, his journey into law enforcement. BJ and I started our law enforcement careers together and that's actually how we ended up meeting.*

Bj and I have been talking about doing a podcast for a few years, and here we are! We are just getting started, brother!

BJAR ATKINS: I'm glad to finally be joining, man. Some of the weather here has not been cooperating as of our original start time. I'm glad to finally get in here and get on this thing and I'm excited about it.

STREET TALES: *Bj is still actively involved in law enforcement down in Florida. Bj had to deal with Hurricane Milton and Hurricane Helene and was basically grinding out 12-hour shifts for sometimes, over a week, 10 days, 12 days. Can you talk a little bit about that?*

BJAR ATKINS: We had to deal with some hurricane stuff out here and obviously being out there in that is, par for the course, a part of the job. That's something that's always understood between, friends, family. They have all gotten the call saying, "Hey, I am not going to be able to make it, work stuff going on, lol."

STREET TALES: *That's the nature of the business. When these things happen, you kind of just prepare because you know what's coming. You always try to hope for the best but plan for the worst.*

BJAR ATKINS: I don't think it's talked about enough and it's not necessarily a complaint, but I don't think people actually think about that stuff when you've got first responders that are helping with recovery efforts, rebuilding efforts, cutting down branches, trees, getting people out of their houses, helping people move out. Because you're doing all of that, you can't take care your own house, your own property, even though you also have your family, your friends, your significant others.

You're trying to make sure that they're good while also doing your job and helping the citizens. Most citizens are waiting for you to respond and help them but very rarely do they stop and think that we have families and friends that are looking to us for help as well. I think every cop is worried about their family and making sure they're good even while they're trying to do their job.

STREET TALES: *I'm not like a super crazy doomsday prepper, no, but I am a prepper. Somebody who takes preparedness somewhat seriously. I'm the kind of guy who always has two of everything just in case this happens. Obviously, we live outside of the scope of the normal everyday citizen in the sense of what we see and experience.*

What happens in society from the top to the bottom, outside the normal top to bottom of the social economics, we see all of it. You get to see a little bit of everything especially in a county as large as Hillsborough, FL.

BJAR ATKINS: When things get really bad, it'll be hard for most first responders to not abandon their duties to go take care of their own families. It's crazy to think about. Can you imagine you're helping everyone else during a natural disaster only to find out your family is in danger or hurt? That's the reason I like taking precautions and being prepared in the event something catastrophic happens.

Growing Up and My Journey into Law Enforcement

STREET TALES: *Absolutely, man. We would have been remiss if we didn't at least address that a little bit. Let's talk about your background and growing up a little bit.*

BJAR ATKINS: I grew up middle class-ish, with a public-school education. I'm born and raised in Tampa, Florida. A lot of my experience has been here in Florida. Florida is a diverse state with many types of cultures, socio economic classes, and, of course, sports dominate in almost every facet of life here!

I just had my 20-year high school reunion not too long ago and thinking back on it, I was different back then.

I was in the gifted program back in the day and even though it was a diverse area, I never actually had another black kid in my class until I got to high school. That was a little bit of a strange thing, thinking back on it now. I actually went from playing sports in high school, baseball, football, basketball. I consider myself to be an athlete to this day, you know. No one can tell me otherwise.

I actually ended up going to USF my first year and then transferred to Grand Lake State in Louisiana. I spent a year out there. Then ended up transferring to Cookman, another HBCU in Daytona Beach. And

I finished out my time there playing football. Obviously like all of us do, once college is over, we're all just starting to figure it out. I moved back to Tampa, FL, where I was born and raised.

I got my first full-time, big boy job working for Foot Locker Inc. One of my very good friends, and her fiancé at the time, was a manager at Foot Locker and hooked me up. I always had an interest in law enforcement and that's why I got my degree in criminal justice.

But at the time I was like, *I don't know if that's what I actually want to do in the long term.* I ran from it a little bit. As a kid, I was always very into comic books. I was and still am a big comic book nerd. I love all of it, Marvel, DC, whatever. Three of my favorite characters are Spider-Man, Black Panther, and Batman. Batman is probably my favorite because he was a normal guy, wasn't just born with innate super powers, but had to work hard, train, and he was smart.

They all had the physical attributes, right? So, I kind of gravitated to that. I said when I was a little kid, "When I grow up, I want to be Batman. I don't have a billion dollars, but I can train my body and educate myself." The law enforcement career is the closest I could come to being a real-life Batman. The World's Greatest Detective kind of vibes, you got the utility belt, you get to chase down bad guys, and you have to solve complex crimes on occasion.

I was doing the champs thing. I was also working as a mover on the side, on the weekends. I had a college degree and here I was working in a stock room, being a mover on the weekends, moving people's furniture, and I realized working these jobs that it was not the path to success for me.

I was always told, go to school, get good grades, graduate, get a good job. But I started to see that maybe that isn't the only way to be successful. We both decided the same thing, I guess, to venture into the law enforcement thing. As you said before, that's how we met, in the academy.

It's kind of been off to the off to the races since then. I've enjoyed my time in law enforcement, and it has been very fulfilling. Obviously, there'll be ups and downs in anything you do in life in any organization, in any job. Putting that part to the side, it has been very fulfilling.

Interactions with Law Enforcement:

STREET TALES: *Growing up, did you ever have any interactions with law enforcement, middle school, high school age, and what were those interactions?*

BJAR ATKINS: I did have interactions with law enforcement growing up and I never had a negative experience. I was pulled over a couple of times, got tickets, but I've never had an experience where I felt, *this will change my view of the profession.*

I've gotten tickets where the officer wasn't the politest, but I never felt like it was because of anything derogatory. Maybe that guy was just having a bad day, you know?

But some of my fonder memories of law enforcement growing up was that in high school, I was in the what I think they called crime watch or something like that. That was my first actual regular dialogue with someone in law enforcement, our school resource officer, Nate Johnson. And that's another full circle story. We'll get into it another time.

I've never had a negative interaction per se. For the most part, my experiences have always been positive. I don't necessarily know of anybody that I know closely personally that has had negative experiences. Not to say that they don't happen because obviously they do, but...

It was never really a thing until I started working in law enforcement to kind of get some of those stories.

STREET TALES: *I hear you and everyone's upbringing is a little different. That's why I try to explore that every now and again. But let's jump into law enforcement academy, and I've kind of touched on that a little bit. What do you recall from those first few weeks of training because I remember it being pretty horrific for me, but I was coming from a bit of a different background.*

BJAR ATKINS: We both played sports, and we both played college ball. For the first two weeks of paramilitary, I didn't take it seriously, but I wasn't shell-shocked. I was actually surprised to see some of the people in our class be shell-shocked by that. It was very strange to me that they would be.

They were just freaked out. I'm thinking, *all they're doing is yelling. Nothing's happening. No one's touching you. You're not in danger. What's going on here?* But now, looking back, I see the purpose for that because it did weed some people out, and rightly so. I get the necessity for it.

I always thought that that was quite funny. I think the overall training academy experience wasn't that much different than college. It was like, you got to do some cop training and some physical training. Basically, what we've been doing our entire lives pretty much. If you come from that type of athletic background, you've got to practice.

I was only like a year removed from college. It wasn't really difficult to fall back into that process. I thought it was good overall training at the time.

In many ways, we weren't trained very well. I mean, obviously there's a lot more to be said about overall training. We've touched on this in our time in enforcement. We could do a whole episode on that by itself, but I think it was a good baseline for initially training. I think there's a lot of things that go into the job that aren't necessarily addressed in the academy per se at the beginning that probably could and should be. But you, you're painting with a very wide brush and you know, you're expected to do a lot with a little. I kind of get why it is the way that it is.

Police Academy

STREET TALES: *Back when we went in, they did a two-week paramilitary style where you went and lived on the training base. You were separated, in my case, from my children and my family and basically went from working bankers' hours to up all hours of the day. I keep saying paramilitary because BJ and I just went to my son's Marine Corps graduation, and we got to see some of the drill instructors and the recruits there and what they were dealing with and the drill instructors screaming and hollering and running. Some of the stories my son was telling, I thought, I will never ever compare myself to Marine Corps bootcamp. I understand the concept. You're taking somebody who's not used to one being treated that way, especially kids who are 17, 18, 19 years old.*

I think they had a couple of 20-year-olds. For the most part, nobody has been subjected to being awakened at 4 a.m. with someone screaming in your face, throwing on shorts, and going for a five-mile run or hike, or whatever. Then the intro level into law enforcement with people yelling at you that people want to kill you. There are bad people. There are evil people. Again, I think at some point we're going to do an episode just on training, just to talk about the different aspects of training. You get awakened to a world where most of us were not criminals or not in the criminal element before going into law enforcement. You're now exposed to saying people want to hurt you just because of who you are, what you represent, the uniform you're wearing. You need to be turned on at all times. It's hard for a lot of people, I'd say everybody, to differentiate, hey, this traffic stop, you're just someone having a bad day, caught speeding, making an illegal U-turn.

Or are they nefarious and they're trying to set you up, and they want to shoot you when you walk up. A lot of people, when they get pulled over, it's usually most people's interaction with law enforcement. They're like, the dude's such an asshole. *That individual officer is trying to ascertain whether or not you want to kill him or her., It's an eye-opening experience. We were unaware that that existed. There was the constant reminder of that. We began to think* okay, maybe they're saying all this stuff for a reason.

BJAR ATKINS: A lot has changed due to social media. It was not as big as it was when we first started law enforcement, right? The constant things that people are seeing and have the ability to say or give their opinions on. It's a lot more readily available now than it was when we first started, right? I remember some of the videos that we saw.

Going to college is typically where you experience people from all walks of life and get exposed to more of the world. Then you have the news where you get a cultivated message. Social media is a game changer and now you're getting a combination of cultivated news and a multitude of perspectives. It also gave rise to different types of law enforcement platforms like the officer down page.

You see how often law enforcement professionals die in line of duty. It's crazy to think it's almost one officer down per day. This is actually dangerous, what I'm doing. I mean, it is a job, but it is a very, very dangerous job.

If we're fighting, is this person trying to hurt me or they're trying to get away? Even when young people come into question, I say, "Hey, you're going to get into fights because people are one scared or frustrated. They're not in their most rational state of mind.

They're in some sort of crisis. They're probably at a low point. You know what mean? They're not necessarily wanting this to be taking place. Nobody wants to go to jail. Some of these things are just the natural reaction to what's taking place is not necessarily always personally you per se."

I've never felt like somebody wanted to kill me or fought me because they disliked me personally. know what mean? I've never experienced that or seen or felt that way, but we obviously did it in our own shit. You know what I mean? But if I'm rationalizing it, like, *okay, yeah, this guy's fighting us because he doesn't want to go to jail. But I'm not saying, hey, this guy might be trying to hurt you or might be trying to kill you because he doesn't want to go to jail.*

I'm on the bomb squad. I've been in bomb tech for the last six years. People will ask, "How do you do the bomb thing? Are you afraid? Are you scared?" I answer, "Well, let's take into account everything that goes into law enforcement. The bomb training, at least on this side, I know exactly what I'm doing. It's possibly an explosive device. If I don't do these things, most times, nine times out of ten, I should be okay. Or we have other ways to do it. It's not an arrest. It's not a very dynamic situation most of the time. Is it dangerous? Yes, of course, but it's not split-second decisions where the most nerve-racking thing I could ever do in law enforcement is a traffic stop. Walk up to a window because, and again, this doesn't matter the area, this doesn't matter the situation, this most number one thing is because yes, this person knows that they're getting pulled over and I don't know who's in the car. I don't know their motives are. That is why you have to be cognizant, right?

This could just be a grandma. This could be a regular routine traffic stop, which most of the time it is. But there is always the chance that this guy's got three strikes. Maybe this guy has two strikes. He's scared to get a third one. Maybe this guy's got a trunk full of dope in the car. He's got a life sentence number of drugs in there or he just committed a murder. Or he just robbed the bank or whatever. Biology wise, people are going to do what they can do to not go to jail or to not be held captive or whatever.

You touched on videos that they showed us in training and just to kind of elaborate on that. What they try to do in training, and again, we can only speak for a couple agencies, is to try to show you what can go wrong when things go really wrong. They have videos that are sometimes open to the public, but of law enforcement getting shot, run over, all these different horrific things that can happen.

Fitness in Law Enforcement

STREET TALES: *I think that they did a pretty good job of trying to walk that line of not just saying, hey, you're basically guaranteed to die. But I don't think that that was the intent. They just wanted you to be cognizant of the dangers involved. It's like, you guys all came from many different backgrounds where most people aren't trying to hurt you. Now that you're in law enforcement, people are going to try to hurt you. Again, not the majority. I think 99% of the time it's routine.*

With that being said, it kind of rolls into fitness and your verbal skills. You touched on it with going to school, being able to talk to people, because again, people can have bad days. People from all walks of life and economic situations and everybody has a bad day. BJ and I were partners off the rip when we got out of training so we dealt with people, actual criminals, gangbangers, dope boys, prostitutes, users, dealers all of that, actual evil people, murderers, pedophiles, things of that nature. But you also need to be able to talk to people who are just like, "Hey, man, I'm just having a bad day.

I just got into a fight with my significant other, my job, whatever. You're catching people usually at their worst. At bare minimum, if you're doing a traffic stop, you're interrupting their day, and they're already pissed at you. Very rarely is it just a, "We're so happy you're here. Thank you for doing your job" type thing. That's a rare occurrence. It happens. But again, you need to be prepared to talk to those people, but not to boost you up too much, but BJ is a large man. We are both large men. He is probably still one of the strongest men I've ever known. I know there's a whole thing about fitness, but can you talk a little bit about fitness and what that looks like and how you think it helps you in law enforcement?

BJAR ATKINS: I think fitness is a very, very big thing in law enforcement, in life in general, but in law enforcement for sure, because obviously your physical fitness level is going to boost your confidence in the sense of knowing, *I can handle myself.*

That will prevent you from doing things out of fear, right? I've always said there's nothing more dangerous than a scared person with a gun because they're unpredictable and they're going to do things based out of fear, not off a reason. They're going to panic, and they're going to do things that they probably wouldn't do if they had the ability to think through it at some point or at a minimum.

If someone's having a bad day or someone's scared or looking for or needing help, when you show up, you need to be able to do something or to be able to help this person. It might be physically, emotionally, maybe sometimes mentally. You need to be strong and confident in all these areas.

You need to be healthy in other areas to have the confidence to be able to do your job well. I've always thought that sometimes the physical fitness standards were a little too low. Maybe this is not in accordance with what the job actually entails. For example, sometimes they're measuring you on running a mile and a half. But at what point in your career do you think you're going to be running for a mile? Maybe you might be sprinting after somebody for 300 meters. I've done that way more times than I've run a mile and a half in my career, way more times. Or being able to physically restrain somebody is important. I've been a 500-pound bencher in my lifetime. I'd say even right now, I could probably still get up 450 on a regular basis. If I don't hold myself to these standards, obviously I don't have any problem showing up to a car and feeling like I can't handle myself. That speaks to something like your wrestling, your grappling, and that kind of stuff. You don't need to be black belt level proficient. I mean, it would help, but you need to be able to know your way around it. We've joked about this too. I feel like one of the first questions people should ask is, *"Have you ever been punched in the face before?"*

That might happen and you need to know what to do if you've never dealt with that. What's more dangerous than a scared person with a gun, right? If you don't know how to react to that, you've never been through any kind of struggle, that's something that needs to be addressed.

STREET TALES: *Male standards as well, right? We've seen it. You can't work out on duty in some cases or in some places They harp on you for working out on company time because what if you get hurt? I get it from that point of view, but at the same time, if I decided to go take my lunch break and sit at Dunkin' Donuts or Krispy Kreme for an hour and stuff my face with donuts, no one's going to say anything.*

BJAR ATKINS: It's definitely my own personal view, but I think that if people are calling for help, you need to be in a position where you can help them. That's where some of my views and background come from because I do take it seriously when that happens.

STREET TALES: *No, absolutely. I've said this before in a couple of other episodes, but there are females, women, in law enforcement that I would go to war with that far exceed most men that I encounter on a daily basis. They have the mindset; they have the physical fitness abilities. But again, sometimes if you get an officer or deputy or somebody in law enforcement that is not necessarily physically fit or who has some sort of physical limitation and they are aggressed verbally or physically, a lot of times it causes them to go to their gun or something like that. It creates more lethal situations than maybe is called for. It's hard to just kind of generalize that because sometimes there's nothing you could do about it. But physical fitness has got to be a standard that is maintained throughout your career.*

BJAR ATKINS: You touched on the mental and emotional. I think that's another thing that's extremely difficult. I think law enforcement has 75, 80, 90% divorce rate. Our supervisors always tell us, when you put that uniform on, you come to work, you got to leave the family stuff at home. Well, that's easier said than done. You're fighting with your spouse, your kids, your kids are going through some stuff or whatever it is. A family member just died, whatever it is.

How Laws are Enforced Differently

STREET TALES: *It's very easy to say, just put that aside and not bring it into the calls or into work with you. It's something that you have to learn to do because it will distract you. You and I have seen, and, in some cases, dealt with how shit can turn bad in an instant, really quick. If you're not locked in, it could go really bad for you. That's a whole other topic.*

BJ and I have dealt with thousands of calls. We went on a run for like two months straight where we were catching armed robbers. We were chasing people through the neighborhoods, and we were racking them up. We had a couple of vehicle pursuits that ended successfully. We had some that did not end successfully, but one of the things that BJ and I would always do is we would sit and talk about life, we would talk about law enforcement. I'm going to bring up one specific time because it stuck with me all these years. BJ and I were not arguing, more debating.

I was saying that laws are not in and of themselves racist or targeted towards low economic individuals. We started talking about pulling people over on bicycles and not having IDs, having lights on their bikes, stuff like that, which was very popular. It was a common tactic used, especially in certain high-drug neighborhoods, where people will run dope on bikes because they don't have vehicles. We knew the statutes off the top of our head. Try to do that in a better part of the neighborhood. BJ said, "Try talking to one of these dudes that are in their bike outfits on their $2,000 race bikes. Do you think those people that are doing these 15, 20-mile rides have their IDs on them? Do you *think they're not rolling through stop signs, and they're adhering to all the rules of the road? "My answer was, "They should be."*

BJ suggested that we go ahead and try that out. I think we got through two stops when my Sergeant called me and said, "What are you doing? Why are you doing that up there?" I asked him what he was talking about. "I'm just doing the same shit I do down in the other part of the neighborhood." He replied, "Stop doing that. Get back to your zone."

I called BJ. I was like, "Dude, you were right, I just got reprimanded because I was enforcing the same laws that we were enforcing in our zone in a more affluent zone." It didn't have anything to do with race. It was more socioeconomic, but that opened my eyes to that type of a policy. You want to elaborate on that?

BJAR ATKINS: I do remember when we were talking about it. I said, "You're right. Laws and statutes in and of themselves are not worded in a racist way or in a way to attack certain social economic demographics. But in the sense of the bike light we're talking about, in and of itself is not racist. But the way you use it can be. That's where the human element comes in. It's open to interpretation."

It depends on who's using it and who's enforcing it and where they choose to enforce it that makes it seem that way. What can get you in trouble is that we see agencies kind of get hemmed up on that. They're only doing that in certain demographics and areas. Then they try to say, "Well, it's because of the area." Words are important, semantics. That's why I said, "Bro, if you try to go up there, it's not going to fly. If you're just doing a double-blind test, apples to apples, you would say, both of these things should end up going the same way." We saw that it's not always like that.

STREET TALES: *We've debated on that premise on different issues as they come up in society plenty of times. It's usually the undertones of things, but I can't quite prove it. I can't quite put my finger on it if that particular law was racist or not.*

BJAR ATKINS: It's not the way it's written, but the way people are using it makes it seem that way. It's one of those eye-opening things.

Different Dynamic Being Black and in Uniform:

STREET TALES: *I'm going to switch gears a little bit because one story is going to kind of tie into the next, but again, you grew up in Tampa and you were in the neighborhood, so to speak, and became law enforcement. Another story was a time that we were working on a robbery. I think it was a carjacking. I can't remember exactly, but it was an armed robbery and involved vehicles. We were in proximity to where you went to school.*

We were trying to do interviews, and as a black man in law enforcement, you get treated a little differently by some people from the neighborhood, especially if they know you. We were with our training officers at the time. People were driving by telling you to chill out, chill out. Do you want to elaborate on that? I remember that we were laughing about that at the time.

BJAR ATKINS: It is a different dynamic being a black man in law enforcement, because the old adage is, *too black for the uniform, too blue for the brother,* right? That's something that I've had to navigate a bit through my career. But that was my first experience with that while in the field.

We were probably a mile away from the high school that I went to, a neighborhood of familiarity. I was going to run into people who I went to school with, or people from the neighborhood or just from the area. I was very surprised. I was like, *oh, wait, that's right. It's still me. I'm just in uniform. I'm doing something professional.* That was the first eye-opening thing, and depending on your perspective, it kind of leans into, how am I going to navigate this? It wasn't like you're a sellout kind of thing. They knew me personally. It wasn't that kind of a vibe, but there have been times when it has been the flip of that. Where it's like you're one of them. I think it's important to have the representation on both ends. You worked with me in that area too. Culturally, I understand what's happening in the neighborhood. But once I finally got over there, the undertone was maybe a little bit racist, but as I kind of got into it further in my career, I see why it's this way.

You went to a Historically Black College University (HBCU). It's like, you're not unfamiliar with black people and black culture. You've been around, you've been immersed in it, honestly.

We understand culturally what's happening in some of these areas. For example, there might be 50 people hanging around in a parking lot. Do they want to trespass or create a disturbance or do something suspicious? We'd go over there and we knew, it's Friday, 7 p.m. Friday. It's just the weekend; people aren't doing anything wrong.

It's a nice outside. The music playing; there's a barbecue going on. What's the problem? Versus someone who's unfamiliar with that altogether, who may come from a different social economic background, a different area, whatever. They might view that differently. We should have someone who's familiar with what's happening over there. I'd rather have it that way.

STREET TALES: *I've had experience with two different side stories when I was playing football at TSU. We were practicing and we were all in matching jumpsuits. We had our windbreakers on, and we were about to get on the bus, but the coach wanted to run through some drills. We were on the Tennessee state campus and next thing we know, four Nashville Police Officers began swarming in, jumping out like there was a gang fight going on. We stopped and the coach was like, "Hey man, what's going on?" The initial minute or two, the cops were like, "What the fuck's going on?" Our coach explained that we were just a football team and we were about to load the bus. The police had gotten a call saying that there was a gang fight going on. They looked at us. I don't know what movies you watch, but gangs usually don't wear all matching blue and white windbreakers and do synchronize drills.*

Jumping into racism in the modern age, do you remember the fight call where you and I had to go speak to this backwoods family in the middle of zone 5 by Orient Road jail?

BJAR ATKINS: There was this kid in the neighborhood, outside. We told him, "We need to talk to your dad about what happened." The kid just turned around and yelled really loud, "Hey, Dad, this colored deputy wants to speak to you." We looked at each other like, *where are we, bro? What year is it? Where are we? What is going on? We're in the middle of Tampa.*

I remember being immediately, immediately enraged. I don't know if I got outside my body for a second or what was happening with me that day, but I remember being immediately offended. I've been called all kinds of things and of all the things that I've ever been called in my life and in my career, that wasn't even close to the worst thing. I don't even think he was trying to be disrespectful. He probably thought he was being polite by saying colored and not saying black or not saying the N word or anything that he perceived to be derogatory. I don't know why that made me so mad. I just looked at him, and he was like, "Man, you've got to handle this. I'm going to sit on top of the program because I knew where I was at the moment and this was not going to play out well." I needed you to handle that one.

You were there a bunch of times when I got called the N word or they would call you a cracker People just want to rile you up, I guess, I don't know.

Losing a Deputy/Friend/Confidant:

STREET TALES: *I want to touch on the deputy/friend/confidant that you lost recently if you are willing to talk about it?*

BJAR ATKINS: I was kind of going through some other stuff at the agency, and I didn't really have you to kind of lean on. You decided to up and leave me there by myself. I wanted to feel safer. I wanted someone else to lean on per se. Through the course of things, I ran into "Abbey" Abigail Bieber. She was somebody I was able to talk to and kind of lean on not just about the law enforcement stuff but life in general the way you and I talk.

She was a very good and very close friend, very close to me. She ended up being murdered by her boyfriend at the time. That was a big blow to everyone, her family, to other people that knew her. For me, it was a very big blow. Dealing with that was a huge test on the mental health side of it.

To the point where, for at least a good year, I didn't want to go into the zone. I didn't want to go into the district. I've been going to therapy for a very long time, even before this took place. This was January of 2022.

I kind of really had to lean into the therapy part, lean into the mental health part. To take it even more seriously than ever before.

You still have to show up to work even when things are not always ideal in your personal life or in your professional life. You still have to show up to work and maintain the same bearing, the same level of professionalism. You can't let those things seep into the way you're doing your job. Obviously, that's a lot easier said than done. I think about it a lot. I think about her pretty much every day, if not every other day. We law enforcement officers are still people too. We still have things going on and need to take mental health very seriously. I go to therapy once a week. I talk about it on some of my other platforms. People who know me personally know that I'm like, "Hey, I can't come out this afternoon. I got a therapy session. Or I need a day." I take this thing seriously. I think it's not only the mental health part of it that is key to just the overall quality of your life, but obviously the overall quality of how you're doing your job and the quality of the product that you're giving to people when you step out of the car.

STREET TALES: *I remember talking to you during that time and the story of how it all went down. It's something, if you're interested, you can look up, but the story itself was heartbreaking. Then I know there is some internal stuff that we won't ever talk about on here, but you know, what was that like for you going back to work, knowing that she was not going to be there again, losing your zone partner?*

BJAR ATKINS: Yeah, I know, obviously, time heals all wounds, but some of us deal with it differently, in the course of time. There are phases of things as they happen to take place. Not having that person to talk to, having the confidence on a daily basis is probably the bigger thing. I miss my friend. I still have things that are going on. I know it affected me at the time and maybe the quality of my work or like when I would think, I *don't really want to be here. I don't want to be proactive. I don't want to write reports. I don't want to take calls. I'm here, not because I necessarily have to be, but I know I have to be here,* but it's not the same level of... *I'm here, but I'm not necessarily here all the way,* if that makes sense.

STREET TALES: *I definitely wanted to bring that up and touch on it. I appreciate you sharing that. I had already been removed and I didn't know her prior, but just from what you've been able to tell me and what you shared with me, how critical she was during that timeframe for you. But, brother, I've had you on for a little over an hour, and I know that it's not the only episode we will do. We've got much more to discuss. I appreciate you. I love you, brother. Stay safe. I appreciate everyone for listening. Bj, thank you so much.*

Story Recap

Bj's path was different from mine and yet the comradery and friendship have stood the test of time and many trials and tribulations. Bj grew up in the city of Tampa, FL, and his athletic and academic career took many paths which eventually led to the law enforcement profession. Timing, fate, divine intervention, whatever it was, the world aligned and we ended up in the same training/recruiting class and were able to watch each other's back and help each other in our individual career paths.

The Story of Bjar Atkins

Click or scan the QR Code
to hear the podcast interview

with **Monique "Mo" Greco**

The Story of
MONIQUE "MO" GRECO

Retired Hillsborough County Sheriff's Deputy Monique "Mo" Greco was trainer, undercover detective, and mentor to Bj and I. Bj and I were newly minted deputies working in the Fish Bowl, District 1, in Hillsborough County. Mo has been a close friend and mentor to Bj and I for over a decade, and her experience and knowledge helped shape our careers and got us through some pretty dark times.

Mo grew up in Florida, in a family that promoted hard work and education. She is the first and only person in her family to choose a career in law enforcement. As a black female, she is definitely unique in the field of law enforcement. Growing up, she was aware of the stigma affiliated with law enforcement and the black community and heard stories from her friends and family about being pulled over simply for being black. Instead of being deterred by this, Mo wanted to make changes from within, thus began her focus and path for her life to become a law enforcement professional.

Mo started as a patrol deputy, as almost everyone does, when starting their law enforcement career. She was exposed to domestic violence calls, drug-related calls, deadly crashes, murders, and calls so horrific they rarely make the news or are spoken about. Mo bounced around in her career from patrol, community outreach, undercover work, and training. She found her calling in the training section and has continued to strive to educate and train the up-and-coming generations of law enforcement professionals.

Mo is now dedicated to breaking the stigma of mental health in the law enforcement community and is an amazing person.

Below is one of many conversations between me and Mo:

LAW ENFORCEMENT JOURNEY &
Lessons with Mo

STREET TALES: *I've got my friend Mo on the line. I met Mo when I was with Hillsborough County. She had been well into her law enforcement career. I was still relatively new. Me and my buddy BJ, who was on a previous episode, were working in an area we call the fifth bowl when we met Mo, and it was probably one of the greatest years of law enforcement in my life.*

Mo helped guide us through not just law enforcement, but also the inner workings of the sheriff's department and the hurdles that you might have to overcome as you progress in your law enforcement career. We are going to be talking about her early life, what got her into law enforcement, and her time as an undercover detective. She was an instructor and has a vast knowledge base and experience within law enforcement.

MO GRECO: Thank you, Tyler, for having me. I've been super excited about doing this since Tyler told me that this was something he was getting involved in and asked if I would be part of it. I have thought about all the different things that we could talk about, all the different experiences that we had. Like he said, we had a great time when we were out there at the sheriff's office together.

I grew up in Hillsborough County, Tampa. That was where I was born and raised. My parents moved there in the eighties. They moved into an area called Town and Country, which was a pretty affluent back in the day. By the time we became cops, it really wasn't anymore. It was a fluent area. I had an interesting upbringing because Mom and Dad, they're still married to this day. I had two-parent household, but when they moved us in the neighborhood, their goal was to move us into a good area.

They hoped that their kids could be raised in a great place with good schools, et cetera, et cetera. And with that being said, we moved into a neighborhood where there were only three black families in the entire neighborhood. Everybody else was white, not even Hispanic. It was just all white. A little bit of a different upbringing in that respect because people look and they think, oh, the eighties, you know, really not a lot was going on. But I would tell you we were definitely viewed as different. When we went to school, we had people who would say things like, "Can I touch your hair?" Because they hadn't seen black people. People weren't doing full-on things like burning crosses in people's yard, but definitely putting out things that would be racially charged to make sure that the three families that were there knew they weren't that welcome.

My background was like that growing up in a predominantly white neighborhood, going to predominantly white schools, and being a bit of the minority at that point and throughout my whole life. With that, I know that my dad struggled, because again, there were so few black people in the neighborhood. My dad was a longshoreman, so he worked very hard and he worked out, and he would run, and do things like that. He had interactions with law enforcement because he would be working out or exercising, jogging, and getting stopped by cops because they thought he didn't belong there. Just to give you that kind of background with me. Overall, I will say I had a great childhood. I didn't have any issues. My parents stayed married. They worked very hard to try to make sure we did get everything we needed and some of what we wanted. I would categorize this as a little bit spoiled but not too crazy.

I was kind of the nerd. I didn't get a letter for sports, I academically lettered, so that's how I got my letterman jacket, because of my GPA. I originally was applying to go out of state for college, but my parents, they did what they could do to take care of us, but they didn't have a lot of extra money. College was an extra expense that we had to figure out, which meant a lot of loans and a lot of trying to get grants and scholarships and things like that. Because when you get into the academic side of lettering, while it's great, you don't necessarily have as much access to all the scholarships. You've got to be the top 1% a lot of times to get scholarships for those kinds of things.

I ended up settling on going to University of South Florida, which was a local college here at the time. At the time it was a very much a commuter college, nothing like it is today. People who went to USF mostly stayed here, locally. It was a great school, but it wasn't like the University of Florida or Florida State where you had the big football teams and things like that. They didn't get a football team until many years after I left. I attended straight out of high school, went into the four-year college. I actually went to school originally under a pre-med major, because I wanted to be a doctor and did three years at USF working towards that degree. I hated every minute of it. It was the end result I was excited about, but I hated the chemistries and the biochemistry. There was nothing about it that interested me. I actually took a year off USF.

While I was off on that year, I still took classes over at HCC. One of the classes that I took was intro to corrections. It was taught, at the time, by a lieutenant with Hillsborough County Sheriff's office. He said to his class, "Hey, if any of you guys are interested in doing a ride along, I'd be able to facilitate you doing that with my squad." Back in the day, I was thinking, this is going to be awesome. It's like cops, but I get to like ride in the car. It's real life. I'm dating myself a little bit, but *Cops* was the big show back then. We didn't have live PD and all the stuff they have nowadays. I said that I would love to do it. I literally did a ride along in his class because, 1., I took his class; I thought it would be an easy A, and 2., I thought it would be fun. I did the ride along, a midnight ride along, midnight shift. I was exhausted, but I remember getting out of the car that night and thinking, *This is it. This is what I want to do.* At the time, I was not only going to school, but I was working a full-time job over at Capital One. I was an account supervisor there or I might've been just a customer service rep. I remember getting out thinking, *I don't want to sit in an office for the rest of my life.* I started really rolling it around in my head and did a little background search on it and thinking this isn't a job that you can just do on a whim.

Family Interactions with Law Enforcement

STREET TALES: *Mo, you were talking about your family growing up and the interactions they had with law enforcement and kind of how that jumped into your head when you were doing ride alongs.*

MO GRECO: Yeah, after doing the ride along, like I said, I really thought this is a job I think I'd like to do, but I knew this was not something you can just jump in lightly, to be a cop. I really did some soul searching and thought, *What would be my purpose?* This gets into a little bit of my philosophy when it comes to being a cop. I'll talk about this when I instruct people. I always tell them it has to be more than *I just want to help people* because that will go away.

Because you'll get tired of quote/unquote "helping people" because you realize that sometimes you don't help people in this job. You've got to have a purpose that's a little bit more than that. I didn't know that. I didn't have that philosophy when I first did this, but it's something that has evolved over time. However, I knew in the beginning this wasn't something that I could take lightly and jump into. I started doing some soul searching, and it came back to kind of the forefront of my mind some of the interactions that my father had had when he would just be out jogging in our neighborhood.

Cops would stop him and say he didn't belong in that area and do things that bordered on racism or abuse. It wasn't right. That's the reality. It just simply wasn't right. Then there were uncles and different people who had had interactions with law enforcement. I thought to myself, *Wait a minute, let me think about the interactions I have had with law enforcement.* I didn't recall seeing a lot of them that looked like me.

To give you some background, at the time, I had dreadlocks that were probably down about waist deep. I was like, what better way for people to look at law enforcement a little bit differently if then that first look, that person looked different than what they were used to seeing. The other thing I really did some evaluation on is if you don't like how things are, you cannot sit on your porch and gripe about it and say, "Yeah, you know, things should be different. They should do this. They should do that." If you don't have a seat at the table, you're unwilling to take a seat at the table. When I thought about it, I thought if I wanted something to be different about law enforcement, then I had to be part of law. That's never been something I will say in my culture that a lot of people encourage their children to do. It's not very commonly encouraged. Let me put it that way. There are some, but it's not a common encouragement where people say, "Hey, you should be a cop," when it comes to my culture.

In my family, I am the only cop that has ever been in my family ever. I enjoyed the ride along immensely. Then when I tacked on these other core principles, I felt it was what I needed to do. I did a couple more ride alongs. I didn't just jump right in at that point. I asked the lieutenant if I could do a few more ride alongs.

He was very supportive. He let me ride along with his squad I think a total of four or five times, and I thought, *Yup, I'm doing it.* Now I had to tell my mom that I wasn't going to go back to school and be a doctor and I was going to be a cop. It was rough. It was a rough road at first because again, it's not something culturally accepted in our family. A doctor was much more on her radar than being a cop. However, I ended up going into the academy, and completed the academy. She watched how hard I worked because I was working full time at Capital One. I went to the academy full time, and because I did not want to spend a year working towards this goal, I buckled down for those four and a half months. I'd go to the academy from eight to five. I would work from six to midnight every day. Then on Saturday, I'd work a 10-hour shift and make up all my hours.

Law Enforcement Academy

STREET TALES: *I'm going to jump in. This just shows you the difference in the Academy time, because when I went to the Academy, it was basically a full-time job, and you got paid to go through the Academy. You're saying when you went, did you have to pay to go to the Academy or did they still cover that part for you?*

MO GRECO: No, I had to pay to go to the academy. I had to buy all of the equipment that was only useful if I became a cop and I had no job waiting for me when I finished.

STREET TALES: *Interesting. I didn't know that.*

MO GRECO: That is why I could not afford to give up my job at Capital One because not only did I need to work through the Academy that four and half months, but I needed to make sure that I had money to pay bills until I got a job. And it took me a while to get hired after I finished the Academy.

STREET TALES: *Really? Was Hillsborough the only place you applied to or did you apply to others?*

MO GRECO: Oh no. I applied a lot of different places. Actually, Hillsborough was my first choice, and I will tell you why. When I said that my family had experiences with law enforcement that weren't always that positive, my family always commented that most of the time, the Hillsborough County Sheriff's Office acted in a really distinguished manner when you compared it to some of the other local agencies that they had in the West. Typically, if Hillsborough came after you, it was because you really did something bad, but they weren't going to treat you like a jerk.

Hillsborough was my first choice because I felt like they were already ahead of where I thought we should be as a law enforcement community. I thought it would be nice to help continue that path to get better. Because like I said, I wanted to make a difference in respect of how law enforcement policed, how people interpreted law enforcement, that kind of thing.

Back at the time when I applied, St. Pete did not have a great reputation, but I thought again, I could make a difference there. I applied at City Police Department. I applied at TPD, St. Paul Police Department. I applied at, I'm trying to remember because it was a long time ago, I'm not going to tell you when cause it's a long time ago, but I applied at probably like eight or 10 different ones. I kind of stopped there because I didn't want it to seem like I was just shotgun blasting.

But I got offers from St. Pete. I got offers from Kansas City, and I got an offer from Hillsborough. Later on, some of the others called, but I had already accepted the job at Hillsborough.

STREET TALES: When you started with Hillsborough, did you start to go through FTO? When I went through, we went straight from the Academy, then we went straight into FTO.

MO GRECO: Yes, but we were in the classroom for about a month. Then after the month-long training in the classroom, you rolled out to the street and did four months of FTO training. You were permitted to be accelerated. I didn't do the full four months. I was accelerated because I was taking this super seriously as a career. It was not something I was going to do for a little bit.

That's what led me to the Sheriff's Office.

STREET TALES: *Mo, you were talking about the work you were putting in during the academy and how your mom noticed the amount of work you did, but you said your dad had some reservations about the change in career path.*

MO GRECO: Correct. I understood his reservations too, because of his interactions with law enforcement. But by the time I completed the academy and I explained to him the whys and he saw the work I was putting in, when I actually got hired on at the sheriff's office, my dad actually penned my badge for me. Super important to me. That was a big deal. I think that was when I really started to see where I was going to make a difference. I think my dad saw somebody that looked like him that was going to be different than the other cops that he had to deal with. Fast forward, I finished the academy. It took me a year to get hired on.

Back then, there were very few females. There were definitely very few black females that were in the academy. Lo and behold, I landed at the sheriff's office and started my career there.

I will tell you from the day I started to the day I left; I always loved what I did. I always loved my job. That part of it. Did I love some of the politics and some of the things that happened in the background? No, but I definitely always loved what I did and stood by what I did. I encourage people to go into this job and do it with a level of excellence because it is a really good job. It's afforded me a lot of opportunities in life.

Subsequently, I started out on the road. I worked the road for a while and I became a field training officer. That's where I got my first toe in and dipped my feet in the pool of training and started realizing I really did like teaching people how to do this job as safely as possible. What is it fundamentally? Something that are the fundamentals of what's going to make you a good cop because I think sometimes it's misconstrued that you got to be able to shoot, you got to be able to this, you got to be able to that. But I will tell you the first and foremost fundamental thing you have to know how to do in this job is communicate. You have got to be able to talk to people because if you cannot talk to people, your career is going to be long and arduous. That's the reality.

Gucci Squad

STREET TALES: *I will say that something you learn pretty quickly is that you have to have the ability to talk to people, and you have to have the confidence that you know what you're talking about. One of my early supervisors, who's still there, would constantly teach us and explain to us, that this is a profession. You need to be confident on what you're investigating, confident in the law, which gives you confidence when you're speaking to someone, whether it's a suspect or a victim.*

That will help you know what you can do. I think a lot of cops and people in law enforcement that get put into these weird situations are kind of unsure as to what they're doing. Potential suspects can read that on you. It's an interesting thing that I don't think that gets talked about enough, but before we get back into training, what was your early career like? Where were you patrolling and what was it like for you?

MO GRECO: I started out, they called us the Gucci district because I started out in district three. We were in an area that was considered a little more affluent than some of the other areas. We had some very, very expensive neighborhoods and homes in our areas, but then we also had some not-so-great areas and gangs and all of the things that you get everywhere else. What I learned from there is that you can be a cop anywhere.

It's just a matter of learning how to be a cop depending on the area that you're in. I started out there, and I worked our area that was deemed the Carolwood area. It wasn't the worst, but it wasn't the best either. My area specifically bordered our next district over, district one, which at the time was probably our worst district. I had a good mix of good and bad. Because they would run over from District 1 right into my zone. It was always a lot of fun. I had an amazing squad my first few years. I stayed with that squad forever. We had a great mix of people, some who had experience, some who were brand new like me, and we all seem to mesh really well. I don't even know if they did it on purpose or if it was something that they were they were mentally thinking that they were doing or if it was just something that was secondary and that was just natural to them because they mentored us to be better cops. Subsequently, we learned how to talk to people and, for lack of better terms, when to hold them, when to fold them, when you're going to need to talk to people, and when you're going need to fight people. It was the ground for me to grow in when I first got out there and it gave me a lot of confidence.

My job forced me to learn a lot of things because the area where I worked had a mix of affluent and not-at-all affluent people. While the calls are different, the treatment should not be different.

My Love for Training and Teaching

MO GRECO: Then I became a field training officer pretty quickly. I was the only midnight FTO and the only female training officer we had in our district at the time. It was interesting and it was a lot because that meant they tried to cycle every new officer into my car because I was the only one that was working at midnight.

There is a definite difference in how you patrol in the daytime versus how you do at night. It's important to learn that. I had a lot of trainees and if you are not well versed in your job, try teaching what it is that you do and it'll bring you up to speed quick. I obviously had to be on my game because these people are coming out and they're asking you questions.

I don't think a trainer has to know every answer, but you better know where to find the answer. That's what I learned very quickly. I was sending these individuals that I trained out with the best and most filled toolbox I could give them at that time. Eventually, they compiled all of our FTOs into a training squad, and we all worked evening shift. I did that for a little while. It gave us the ability to train them on day shift stuff and night shift stuff and be able to collectively have one supervisor we were reporting to. It really was a better system to handle training. After doing that for a little bit, I ended up going to a crime prevention unit.

I think they've changed the name now. It's not called crime prevention anymore, but basically, we were the party planners for the sheriff's office. We planned any type of recognition for the deputies, all types of things where we were speaking with the community, doing a lot of community engagement type stuff. People laughed at us because they didn't necessarily see the usefulness of a crime prevention unit.

But as someone who's been in that unit and worked on the street and done all these things, building those bridges with the community prior to the point when you need them are incredibly important. The agencies that take the time to go out and meet the community when in positives light, when it comes time, when there is that shooting, when it comes time, when there's that something that happens where the community wants to question you as an agency, if you have not established a relationship with them prior to that event, it usually does not fare very well.

That's where I saw the usefulness in what I was doing there, along with the fact that at the time, the sheriff held seats on lots of different boards throughout the community. Obviously, he was one person who can't attend every single meeting. There were many cases where we would represent the sheriff at different boards and things like that. I got to sit on different urban leagues and different types of community boards and have a more intimate understanding of what these people's concerns were, what they liked that law enforcement did, what they didn't like that law enforcement did. I became like a part of the board, so they didn't hold their tongues really. They were speaking pretty freely at that point.

STREET TALES: *You brought up a couple of things. I'm just going to recap, but because it ties into the next part. You talked about there's different ways of law enforcement during the day and at night and having been trained on nights and worked mostly nights, you deal with a lot of in-progress calls for service, things like robberies, domestic, whatever it is that's occurring. You also deal with a lot more drunks, things of that nature.*

You get a wide array of calls. Daytime is usually delayed. But you also ended up working a lot more with detectives. Especially when I left, usually most of the senior deputies would want day shift for personal reasons, personal life, regular sleep schedule, but also, they're kind of progressing their career. I didn't even know you worked for community services, and that's something that's been a hot topic in law enforcement. In my opinion, there's no one way to interact and engage with a community. I think that they're all necessary. I know a lot of things have been tried. It's not always just gone, go, go, get all the bad guys, get them off the street. You need to be able to engage with people who live there because it also develops that relationship where they feel comfortable talking to you.

MO GRECO: When I was in crime prevention, another thing that I thought we did that was amazing is that we were all assigned a certain number of schools to go to and we would teach the confirmation program they would learn from a real deputy who walked into the building in uniform. We would go out to these schools, and we would teach in kindergarten; we would teach them officer friendly. We would teach pedestrian safety and bicycle safety. We did a drug awareness program with the fourth graders. In fifth grade, we did a whole junior deputy program that we would put these kids through. Then, we would see them for maybe four or five sessions and we would give them their junior deputy pageant. While it seems like those are just silly programs and they should have outgrown those kinds of things, they hadn't. I still don't think they have. It's connection. I always made it a point to address myself as Deputy Mo instead of at the time I was Deputy DeVage and when I left, I was Deputy Greco, but I would say I'm Deputy Mo. I became a person to them, not just that uniform.

STREET TALES: *BJ even talks about that, that one of the school resource officers that he had connections with kind of motivated him and made him interested in law enforcement. Then on the opposite side of that, previous people that I've talked to, even though they didn't necessarily go into law enforcement, remembered those interactions with cops, people on the law enforcement side that engaged with them as a human being.*

You know, that's huge. To this day, I still try to go talk to schools and put myself out there because a lot of kids, like you said, have never met a law enforcement officer in a controlled, safe environment, not in uniform, who are, just there to talk to you, let alone a federal agent. It's interesting the questions that pop up and the stuff that they learn from their family or their friends or what they watch on TV. I have to tell them no, that's not a normal occurrence.

MO GRECO: I had two really affluent schools and then I had several that were not so affluent, and kids were kids whether I was in the affluent schools or the regular ones that were not so affluent. They all had curiosity about law enforcement. They all had a curiosity about me as a person. I told you, when I started law enforcement, I had dreadlocks that came down to my waist. But I'm used to wearing them in this big huge giant bun.

At one of my schools, the kids were astonished when I walked in. You know, they thought, she's black. And then several of them were like, *she has dreads*. They were so astonished by that. I remember there was one kid that was struggling in school, and he said, "I want to see your dreads down." I'll tell you what I said. "If for the remainder of the year that I am coming here, your teacher tells me that you're acting appropriately, you're doing well in school, I will come in one day, and I'll eat lunch with you with my dreads down." I said, "That way you can get a chance to see them." Now, I will tell you, sidebar, that was outside of our uniform code. We weren't supposed to do that. But I thought that would have been something that was going to stick with that kid because people don't always remember all the details of what happens with a situation, but they will remember how you made them feel.

For whatever reason, that was something that I think made him feel special that I was doing that for him. He did what he was supposed to do. His teachers have made a huge impact on this kid. I went back, we ate lunch together, I took my dreads down, and it was just, for him, it was almost like he was looking at someone that was a celebrity, because I think it was so out of the box for him to see someone who looked like him, that was wearing this uniform and treating him like a human being, you know?

Going Undercover

STREET TALES: *I understand there needs to be dress code policy and the way you speak and interact. But for most people that you're talking to in a one-on-one setting, it's very robotic and you need to be able to still be a human. We can talk about that because the way you talk to people, we've talked about this, depending on where you're at or where they're at, if you try to speak like a college professor, most people will not respond. It comes off like you're being an asshole or whatever. They just want to hear you talk as who you are, not some robot, because this is how the agency expects you to be. It's like, no, I'm still a human being.*

MO GRECO: I had been there for a couple of years and ended up becoming the liaison for the black advisory council. I'd done that for a little bit and I wanted to get promoted. That's what it boiled down to. They said at this point I needed detective experience. I put in my memo to go to a detective unit, and I landed in what was our star squad at the time. It was a squad that was created kind of like the street crimes unit or green team, and they were there for the whole county. We did a little bit of everything. We did surveillance; we did light undercover work. The idea was that about 5% of the people roughly do a good portion of the crime. If we can try to get that 5%, we can make a real impact on the amount of crime.

STREET TALES: *You're saying the undercover unit was focused on individuals that were recidivists or causing most of the crime? And you mentioned that 5% of the population or 5% of the criminal population, probably more precisely, cause over 95, 96% of the crimes I think the FBI put out some stats that rings true that it's not just all these random criminals running around. It's a very select group of criminals causing the majority of the crime.*

MO GRECO: We were tasked with focusing on those individuals so that we could really make an impact in the overall crime picture essentially. I did that for a little bit and then at about the two-year mark, they decided the star squad wasn't really useful anymore. They disbanded us and we all had to figure out where we wanted to go. We had a couple different options. One of the options was to go fully undercover. I thought, well, I'll try it.

It's not anything that I ever had aspired to do. It was not just that you were working on the street. When I came on, there was the green dot scam when they were basically filing taxes in other people's names. That was pretty hot and heavy when I switched to undercover.

It was a good bit of our focus. My partner and I bought guns like crazy. The sheriff's office always focused on getting guns off the street. We bought as many illegal guns as we could get. We bought dope, but the dope for us was mostly focused on pills. Don't get me wrong. We bought weed and we bought cocaine. We bought crack sometimes, those kinds of things, but pills was really a lot of what we bought during that timeframe.

I bought people's social security numbers. A crazy amount. People would sell me a legal tablet full of social security numbers, my God. With the idea that I was going to be filing taxes and doing those kinds of things. In that job, I also had a bunch of people that, subsequently we work with being an undercover detective. It's one of the few detective positions where you work the case from start to finish.

A lot of our detectives are fed cases because they start out on the street. A street-level deputy responds out and then they feed them the case. Undercover, a lot of times I'm going out, I'm cold buying. Once I've done the cold buy, I then have to figure out who this person is. Cause usually bad guys aren't going to be like, "Oh, good afternoon. This is my first and last name." You got to figure out who they are off of a nickname usually, and then build your case from there. Make the arrest.

Sometimes you can make them a confidential informant and flip them. Other times, you can't and so you end up just taking it all the way to report proceedings. With that being said, I was able to learn the skill set of working with confidential informants and managing CIs is what we call them. Getting them set up, how to keep them safe because once they became a confidential informant it became my responsibility to make sure nothing happens to them in the course of what we're doing. It was very interesting for me, but it was not my cup of tea. It wasn't my ideal job because you realize very quickly you are a bad guy. You have to be in order to do that job. You lie to everybody because you got to lie to CIs, you got to lie to your bad guys, you got to lie to make sure that you're always keeping your story straight. It was really cumbersome for me for that reason. And that was the part I did not like because it was constantly like, *oh gosh, like, what did I tell this person? What did I say to this person?*

What was finally my breaking point where I was like, this is just not for me, I had a CI and at this point she was an unwitting CI. She didn't know I was a cop, but she was introducing me to a lot of different people. She called me one night in the middle of the night crying. I asked her what was wrong. Long story short, her grandmother had gotten very sick and was being rushed to hospital and probably was going to die.

She called me and said, "I'm calling you because you're my only friend, and I just needed somebody to be able to hear me out." I thought, *this lady doesn't even know my real name.* As a human being, it hurt my soul in that moment that person in one of the worst positions of their life, called me they thinking I'm a friend of theirs. I'd been doing nothing but lying to her. You know, it's my job. It's my job a hundred percent. Was she doing wrong stuff? Absolutely.

STREET TALES: *How long were you undercover at that point? Like for deep undercover? How did that affect you with your not job-related friends and family, and did that change you in any way in how you interacted with them?*

MO GRECO: From my perspective, I don't think I did. The only thing I will say it did is it pulled me out of being able to be as engaged with my family because like I said, you're always a bad guy. I had hours that I worked, but the bad guys didn't know I had hours. I got called all the time. It was a little embarrassing sometimes because I'd be at my family's and all of a sudden, my bad guy phone rings.

I'd have to step away because I didn't want my parents to hear me talking or doing this role essentially that I was doing. I wasn't proud of it. That's where it translated to the same situation with the lady. I wasn't proud of the fact that I was somebody that she thought was a friend and I wasn't. I couldn't be and I didn't want to be.

Now, the funniest part is I had a partner that I was partnered with and he loved it. He loved being a UC. He had done it. He had worked for another agency in another state. I think that's what got me through, him being my partner through that time in my career because it was just for me.

That's where I think the human side of me just didn't enjoy those parts of it. It did make me different with my family because I felt like I didn't know if they'd be proud of this part of what I was doing.

Meeting Tyler and Bj, Revitalizing My Passion to Teach

STREET TALES: *These are good points and stuff that I kind of know, but maybe not everybody knows, is that there's such a vast array of ways to enforce the law and it takes all kinds of people. There are so many different crimes. I know I've had discussions because I couldn't care less about traffic crimes, but people really care about that. They love pulling over cars or they love the dope.*

MO GRECO: Buying and selling dope, getting dope off the streets or wherever it is. I don't think it makes you a bad cop or even a bad person. I don't really agree that you can still focus your interest and your skill sets on such a vast array of different types of criminality. There are white collar crimes, robberies, sexual assaults, or things like drug sales/use, obviously is always on the forefront using the media and stuff, but it takes all kinds and I think you don't know that until you start doing the job itself. I know that when I started, I was like super into the robberies and these people crimes, but then I transitioned my interest to other things in law enforcement because you just kind of arrest the same people over and over again. I thought, *am I even making an impact?*

STREET TALES: *You bring up a very good point and I appreciate you sharing that.*

You said that phone call over this lady who felt like you were a friend that was kind of your out point. I did this for a few years; I checked the box. I want to get out. *What was kind of the next stage for you?*

MO GRECO: I had done it because I wanted to get promoted. But I ended up going to my supervisor and saying, "I've been here for a while, quotients are coming up. I'd like to get pushed for promotion." I was basically told, "That's understood. However, the reality is we already have a black female that we're to push, so we're not going to push you this time." That was a bit deflating.

It didn't go well after that. I ended up kind of going through an IA situation and the result was they moved me back to the street. That's where I met you guys. Up until that point, if I worked the street, I worked the midnights and I thought to myself, *I'm going to go back and have fun. I have not been that happy in this role that I've been doing.*

I went back to working midnight patrol and that's where I met you and BJ. And it was definitely reminiscent of my first years of being a deputy because the squad I worked for when I first came on, we had so much fun. And when I came back, it wasn't necessarily the whole squad, but me, you, and BJ out there doing our job, doing it right, being effective.

I'm not one that says, "Well, you can't enforce law because it's not fair." No, we enforced the law, but we had a good time. We enjoyed it. We took care of each other. All those things that I felt like had been a bit lacking.

STREET TALES: *That was just such a good moment for me and my personal and professional career. BJ and I were still relatively new. We weren't held in the best light for our bosses because we were known to get into all kinds of stuff at all hours of the day. We had a very clear mindset on how we felt we should enforce the law and what crimes we wanted to go after. We weren't afraid to get vehicle pursuits and chase people on foot. We did all kinds of stuff, which despite* *popular belief, bosses and supervisors do not like. It causes paperwork headaches and ties up resources. That's the way they view that type of activity. We were in district one, which you brought up before as being like one of the worst districts for crime. It has a very high population of criminals. We were sent down to one of the farthest away areas of district one known as the fishbowl.*

We were told, "You guys are going to get a new zone partner." All we were told is just leave her alone. She's a senior deputy. She'll do what she wants and give her a wide berth was what was described to us. I looked at you like, fuck that, man. We're going to go find you. I don't know how many shifts you actually worked. We were just so busy and caught up, but it probably took a few shifts, a few days. I don't remember exactly the time that we rolled up to say, "What's up, Mo? I'm Tyler and this is BJ." And you responded, and from there, we started backing each other up on calls. You told us, "You guys are crazy." But just like you, we liked to have fun with it. We tried to talk to people and get out and walk the area.

Teaching the Next Generation

MO GRECO: You know what was funny is I came back out and what occurred to me is I had a lot of experiences that had now given me more tools in my tool belt. I had done crime prevention. I worked undercover. I had done the countywide street crime. I thought, *now I have the ability again to go back to what I really like doing, which was teaching people.*

I knew coming to midnight that I was going to be bumping into a lot of people who were going to be less senior than me. When I met you two, I thought, *OK, well, this could be exciting. They are excited about the job still. I want some of their excitement to bleed off on me. But I also see some little things that I can help them with.* There were times where I thought, *y'all don't have to fight just yet.*

I think that was the beauty of my relationship. I was learning from you guys and taking in some of that excitement that had been taken away from me because of the situation and circumstances. I was, in turn, excited to share with you guys how to do this job safer and different maybe than you originally were looking at it.

I didn't know how to feel you guys out. But once I realized, *OK, these are dudes are genuine about what they're doing. It seems like we have the same like mindset like the core at the core values,* I just ran with it. Then when I started sharing with you guys a little bit to say, "Let's try this this way. Hear me out on that," you guys listened. I thought, *this is going to be great. We're going to be really good because I can learn from them and they're willing to learn from me too.*

STREET TALES: *BJ and I talk about it all the time. I'm not going to say specifically just because we played sports, but I think we both have very strong opinions on what is right, what is wrong, and how we want to do things. But there's something about being able to be coachable. I will argue my point and then if you say, I hear you, but this is how we do it, I think, okay, I can learn something new, and I keep it moving. But not only being able to listen, it's about being able to reenact it, regurgitate what I'm being told. It also got me in trouble with some supervisors who were less than thrilled. Plus, BJ and I are bigger people. I'm six four. He's six two. But for bigger dudes, sometimes even within law enforcement, supervisors who are not that size, they feel like you're using your size to intimidate them. You on the other hand, never felt that way or at least, if you did, you never expressed that as an opinion. You were like, I don't give a shit. Cause I'm here and, Mo, I would go to war with you. You would be* *interviewing somebody, BJ and I would stand three inches from their face, just waiting for them to do something stupid.*

MO GRECO: That was why I said we had so much fun, and I think that it balanced us because you guys are big dudes for sure, and I was never intimidated by that. Sidebar, it's because my dad's six four and my brother's six five. That was normal for me and size doesn't ever intimidate me. I never ever wanted you guys to feel like you had to take care of me or I was a liability to you. I made sure that I didn't write checks that I couldn't cash or I wasn't willing to at least cash. I made sure that I did toe the line with you guys. That's why I don't think there was an intimidation factor. I was older than you guys, I still am, but being older than you guys, I never wanted to feel like you guys felt you had to take care of me. I didn't want you thinking she's the girl, she's the old lady, or any of those things. I wanted to bring that to the table along with my wealth of knowledge.

I realized as an FTO, I love teaching people how to do this job and learn from the mistakes that I made. As an instructor, a trainer, an academy manager, all those things, I had no problem sharing mistakes that I made so that you didn't have to make them. I would be the big sister that did all the things so that you didn't have to take all of the lashes that I did. You could just live off of my experiences. At that time, I was probably 12 years in, Andi realized that I was not going to do this forever and wanted to make sure that things were different, make a difference. I wanted to leave a kernel or a ripple effect that then radiates out. Working with you I thought, *I can truly make a difference because I teach Tyler, Tyler teaches somebody else, that person teaches someone else, et cetera, et cetera. That's why I loved our time out on the street.*

I knew that we were all going to be safe, but we were all going to teach each other something. I would interview people and you two would stand there, funniest thing ever to see two of the biggest guys you probably will ever see in uniform and they're literally breathing down someone's neck. I'm like, "No, no, look at me, look at me and talk to me. If you don't do that, then we're going to have a problem. Stay with me, answer the question." The way we interacted with people, they didn't even complain. They were just like, "Okay, here we go."

Cop Stories With Mo

STREET TALES: *I'll bring up one of the stories, talk about holding our own. We responded to a domestic, the father was intoxicated, and when I say intoxicated, I mean, very intoxicated. He was fighting with his two teenage sons, who were known to be affiliated with street gangs. It's not like Bloods and Crips, there's different street gangs, there's all kinds of stuff, but they were also known criminals. There was a mom in there and there was also a young girl in there, and they were actively fighting.*

Mo and I showed up and we pulled the dad out. We went in because the two teen boys were hyped up, had their shirts off, and they were ready to fight. They wanted to fight us. We pulled the dad out and said, "tay outside. Let us go address what's inside. We'll come talk to you. Just stay right here." He said, "I got it. I got it." We went in and the two teenagers looked like they're ready to fight us. We were trying to talk to the mom, who was upset. The little girl was crying. The next thing we know, the dad jumps in. I don't know if he broke through the glass, but he came through a window one way or another.

The two teen boys look over and the dad just dive tackles one of the kids. Mo was ready to go jump in. I pulled out my taser and gestured for Mo to take out her taser. Then motioned to Mo, you take the one on the left and I'll take the one on the right. We did a double taser. I think I ended up tasing the dad. You tased the son that was fighting with the dad and then all hell broke loose for a minute. We ended up arresting the dad and the son that were fighting for domestic. Think the other son, we ended up having to Baker act because he was just losing his mind. The mom was crying.

MO GRECO: I love that story because on an average day, I was always the one to try and not fight or taser folks. But that particular day, I don't know why that one struck a nerve with me. I was like, this is ridiculous. And you were like, no, calm down. You became the teacher and I became the student on that day, lol!

STREET TALES: *I'll bring up another one because again, these are just moments that stood out. You lived in an area that you were also guarding. It was like a state park or community park or something like that. You had trespassers, people going in the woods doing God only knows whatever they are doing. You would get calls for service, there's somebody in the woods where you live. I remember BJ and I both were getting off shift. We heard you call out on the radio that you had two trespassers at your home, and we both turned around and hit lights and sirens to back you up.*

MO GRECO: I got to my house, I heard you go on the radio I think at the time, my husband, who was also in law enforcement was there, but he was going to bed. He had on a white undershirt and shorts or something.

He was running down, we were pulling up and these two individuals, not fully dressed. I think one of them had on elephant underwear for people who know what that is. We just jumped out hot. That was one of those moments where you were like, "It's all good. I got him." I took the one you were talking to and I stood next to him. BJ had the other one saying, "Don't you move." When my husband, Frank, arrived on foot, he saw you and Bj were my back up and made sure I was good before turning around and walking back to the house. The only reason he did that is because you and Bj were the ones backing me up.

Well, that was huge because I lived on a county park, but it was like 1500 acres of biking and trails and things. It was woods essentially. These individuals, as I was driving home, there was a car parked in this dark area of the park. I had to pull over there, and these individuals emerged from the woods as I was in the middle of running the tag from their car. It was just me in the middle of the woods with these two people.

I got on the radio so that somebody knew where I was because if they were to look at our mapping system, it would look like I was home because that's where I lived, essentially. I had such a good working relationship with you guys and I loved it that I didn't have to say I needed backup. You guys could tell by the tone of my voice. You guys were actually logged off and came up on your unit numbers because you were done for the night, technically. My husband, at the time, he was still my fiancé, would never have left me with someone, but you guys, he knew *she's good. They got her.* It was great. It was absolutely great.

I don't know if you remember this one. but I remember we got a call on day shift. At an apartment complex in one of our really bad areas, some lady was screaming for help in her apartment. We got dispatched out on this call a second time and every time we would go there, we were getting no answer at the door. Well, this time, we investigated a little further and the neighbor said there was someone in that apartment. She had been screaming for help for a couple hours.

We were concerned. We did our due diligence, talked to several neighbors, come to find out there was somebody in there. They were pretty sure it was a male and a female and thought that the woman was being held against her will. Long story short, after we tried several ways of trying to get in, we got approval to kick the door in and it was funny because it was just me and you.

In a lot of cases, I would not have hit a door with just one other person, but I knew how we operated and I felt confident in our skillset that we would be okay. You kicked the door in and we ended up going in. There was a girl being held against her will and the husband or boyfriend, had a knife to her throat. When we went in guns drawn, we were able to get her out.

You grabbed him by some part of his body and he got slung around like in the *Avengers* movie. We were able to make a good arrest and be safe about it. You talk about having people that you trust to that level because people think that in law enforcement, trusting your zone partners is innate. It's not, it is something that comes with building a relationship with that person and understanding how they operate. That's the opportunity I got with you and BJ.

STREET TALES: *I don't remember the exact nature of the call, but you just reminded me there was another call. Sometimes you get calls and it's with people who just want to be kind of assholes. They think you're not investigating something the way they want you to. This time it was a lady who said that her ex-boyfriend stole something. She started getting an attitude with you to the point that I started like looking around, under the couch, and behind the curtains.*

We had done these types of calls enough times that you did the same thing. We were looking under chairs and couches, and she said, "What are you guys looking for?" I can't remember it was you and me, but we answered, "We're trying to see who you're talking to. Cause I know you're not talking to me like that. We're here to help you." We kept it together, but after that call, we were dying laughing talking about it.

MO GRECO: Yeah, we had a good time because we talked to people like real humans.

STREET TALES: *I want to tie into what have you been doing post your career and what does that look like for you with your family and the law enforcement string and the experience that you had.*

MO GRECO: After I ended up going back to the street, I subsequently did things backwards. I always tell people, I had a long career, and then I got pregnant and I had my son and with what I had done in this job, if we could afford it, wanted to put him in daycare and keep running and gunning. I realized right away when I got pregnant, I was going to be a different cop and I felt like I needed to shift into a different role.

I realized I had a bug for training. I became a field training officer. I got certified to be an instructor. I had been teaching for a number of years at our agency, as well at one of the community colleges, and at the academies. I taught firearms and general instruction type stuff. That was something I enjoyed. Once I had my son, I decided that I was not going to stay in law enforcement. I had dumped a lot of my eggs into being a trainer and being an instructor because I thought that was where you can really make that ripple effect. I started teaching pretty hard and heavy. Once I left, I moved to a neighboring county and in that neighboring county, they also had a training center.

I started teaching at that training center prior to leaving law enforcement, and they liked the way I ran their program. I did a lot of the firearms teaching at that college and a ton of the in-classroom stuff.

My focus has always been communication and really wanting to teach people those kinds of things. I can teach you how to shoot, you how to fight, how to drive, but what you're going to do every single day as a cop in your career is talk to people.

I don't think they were happy with a lot of the people who were teaching communication. It was kind of just going through the motions. I was one of the few instructors that really jumped into that wanting to approach it with a level of excellence and making sure these kids came out with a skillset. Let me get on my soapbox for a minute.

A lot of the people who are going into law enforcement today have little communication skills because they are growing up in an era where they can do chat GPT, can be on Facebook, Instagram. They have Facebook friends and people that they are on Instagram with, but they don't actually have real interactions with real people. They Instacart their food, they pay for their gas at the pump, they never talk to people. That was one of the things that I was pretty passionate about.

I jumped into doing a lot of teaching on that. In that aspect of communication, I did a lot of the teaching for serving special populations, whether it be teaching them how you deal with people who are homeless differently. How do you deal with people who are drug addicts differently? How do you deal with someone with mental health illnesses? Because that's something that we deal with regularly. I really focused on trying to take the information that the Florida Department of Law provides us as instructors, building it out and showing them how it's really applicable in their real-world usage. Because the book stuff doesn't take me long to teach them.

But showing them how you take that book stuff and overlay it on real world situations is what I like to do with them. I did a lot of that. I taught legal. I taught report writing because that was always something I was pretty strong in. Once I started teaching a lot, the training center must have liked me a lot because they started doing some things differently. I ended up being certified as a defensive tactics instructor, and I got certified as a driving instructor. I taught driving defensive tactics. I'd been teaching firearms and then, of course, all of the general instructions. I was doing that on a very small scale and my husband, who was also in law enforcement, retired about a year and a half after I left. I started teaching more because I knew my son could stay at home with his dad and I felt more comfortable with that. That had been my focus for the first probably five years after I left the Sheriff's office. It was solely focused on being an instructor and teaching the next generation of law enforcement officers what really matters.

About five years after that, they created the college here in the county where I'm at. I was offered a manager position for the entire academy. I managed the law enforcement, the corrections academy. I was overseeing all of the instructors that we had, which was a hundred plus instructors to make sure that they were staying, and that all of their certificates and their certifications were in compliance with the state. I also oversaw all of our advanced and specialized training and then our facilities. We had an actual gun range at our college, and we have a driving pad. Kind of overseeing all of those things was definitely a shift because it moved me out of the classroom. But what it allowed me to do is the thing that I've always liked to do.

I started mentoring new instructors that were going to be going out there and teaching and trying to get into their heads to not just think about delivering the information, but how they could deliver it and engage the student. How can I teach these people that what you're reading in the book, how to take that and overlay it over these real-world situations? The thing I used to always tell them is, "Remember, you're not teaching people a checklist of how to be a cop. If that was all there is to it, we would all walk around with a book and it'd be like, step one tells the person to do this etc. We are teaching them how to think because these situations are going to be ever evolving. We are giving them tools in their tool belt that they can think through looking at a situation. What tools do I need to reach in there and grab whether it be interpretation of law, communication, dealing with a mental health issue, or writing a report? We're teaching them how to think through whatever that situation is that's in front of them on how to do it."

That is what I did up until a little while back. Recently, I took a step down from that position because I left the sheriff's office so I could focus on my son and rearing him and making sure that he grows up to be the man that I would like him to be, what my husband and I morally think he should be. The job was taking up a little too much of my time when it came to it. I've recently taken a step back, and I've gone back to just being an instructor.

I still think that I make an impact when I'm in the classroom and I'm talking to these students and I'm engaging them. I am one of those people that will play a video that is not something that they want to watch but that challenges their way of thinking. I think, as a cop, you have to be open to the evolution of the way you interpret situations. Because if you get stuck in your ways, you are never going to be a good cop, ever.

That's always my goal as an instructor, to teach them how to evolve their way of thinking at all times.

STREET TALES: *You tied it in well, because this is definitely not the last episode. There are additional episodes that are being worked on, going over training. You outlined it perfectly and found out what it takes to be in law enforcement. You can't teach all these things in a four-month or eight-month academy. This is a profession.*

MO GRECO: I just want to say thank you for giving me the opportunity to talk about this because it is needed for those in law enforcement as well as those who aren't in law enforcement.

Story Wrap Up

What can I say about Mo to capture her importance to me in my professional and personal life? Mo is slightly older than I am, has a vast array of knowledge and experience and a passion for teaching. Mo was willing to teach and train me and Bj when she really did not have to and had other things going on in her life. Mo is a badass and an exceptional example that law enforcement professionals can come in any size, shape, gender, or color. The mentality and dedication to learn and grown and then pass on that knowledge is what matters.

Mo has a patient and unique view of law enforcement and her passion to be a trainer is evident within in moments of meeting her. Mo has always encouraged me and supported me professionally to the point she is now co-hosting the Street Tales Podcast with me! Mo pushes everyone around her to be a better version of themselves and has never expected anything in return. Mo is an exceptional person and for any women interested in pursuing law enforcement as a career, she is an excellent role model!

The Story of Monique "Mo" Greco

Click or scan the QR Code
to hear the podcast interview

with **Adam "Mac" Macaluso**

The Story of
ADAM "MAC" MACALUSO

Adam "Mac" Macaluso and I met while completing the Firearms Instructor Training Program and the Federal Law Enforcement Training facility in Glynco, GA. In meeting Adam, I learned about his life as a Marine Corp Lieutenant Colonel where he led young men in combat during the U.S. invasion of Afghanistan, becoming a Special Agent for the Department of State, then later, a local cop in New Jersey. He now works as a school security officer.

Adam has suffered immeasurable loss and had experiences very few individuals can even begin to imagine. Adam is an amazing man, husband, father, Marine, and law enforcement professional. His story is wild, chaotic, poignant, and touches so many aspects of the soul. I truly appreciate his willingness to be vulnerable and truthful about his experiences and desire to share them with me.

Below is a conversation with Marine Corp Lt. Col. Adam Macaluso and I:

FACING WAR AND LOSS:
An Interview with Marine Corp
Lt. Col. Adam Macaluso

STREET TALES: *I'm excited to speak with an exciting guest who has a vast array of experience in the military, federal law enforcement, local law enforcement, cyber, and has seen combat. He's a recently retired lieutenant from the Marine Corps. Adam Macaluso worked for the Department of State and worked at the Ramsey police department. Adam has a vast array of experience working with foreign militaries, foreign law enforcement, and protecting various foreign ministers.*

ADAM MACALUSO: Thanks, man. I appreciate you having me on, bro. I look at this as a big honor. Thank you for having me on the podcast, and I'm psyched man.

STREET TALES: *You have amazing fucking stories and just getting to know you over last few weeks, I had to get you on the podcast, and I'm excited to get into it.*

ADAM MACALUSO: I was never a big podcast guy, but when you asked me to be on the podcast, I started listening to podcasts and of course show support to my buddy!

STREET TALES: *The big thing for me is capturing people's stories and experiences. I'm always excited to discuss people's lives, experienc-*

es, and passions. I always learn something new and hopefully people have the same feeling that I do!

I'd like to start off with the how someone's upbringing leads them into a life of military or law enforcement service. In your case, you did both. Can you talk a little bit about your upbringing and what that looked like?

ADAM MACALUSO: I had a weird upbringing coming from an upper middle-class family. My dad was a retired doctor. I grew up in a decent house, my mom didn't work, and I have a brother and a sister. I had always been fascinated with the military. I always loved it. My dad was not in the military. The only person in my family that was in the military was my grandfather who passed away before I was born. My grandfather was a doctor too, and he fought in World War II. It's weird because my dad never tried to steer me away from it. My mom wasn't crazy about it. My dad just wanted me to get a good job that pays well. He didn't care if I was happy or not. He would say, "Get a good job so you can pay all of your bills." With that being said, he was always pretty supportive of my career choices. My mom, on the other hand, did not enjoy the military career path.

My dad was a really smart man, and he passed that on to my sister. He went to med school in Italy, and he went over there not speaking the language. He completed med school, while learning Italian. I would have never been able to do that. My brother was an OK student. My sister was a straight A student. Then there was me, I graduated high school with like a 1.9 GPA.

I bounced around to different colleges and worked odd jobs. I was still very immature, I was into the partying scene in college, I just wanted to party and that's it. I didn't care about school. I remember it was a few years in and I think it got to the point that I was pissing my dad off. My dad said, "I'm paying for four years of school for each of you, and that's it, no more, no less." My dad realized I was just putzing around and had no real direction.

At one point, my dad sent me financial aid forms to drive the point home. I will say my dad is a man of his word, because my sister ended up going to law school and she had to pay for the law school portion of her education. My parents weren't horrible or anything like that, and I stayed with them for a large portion of my college time, but I needed direction and wanted a life and that is what pushed me into the direction of the Marine Corp.

I did finish college, which meant I joined as an officer in the Marine Corp instead of enlisted. My friends and my family thought I was being stupid when I told them. I never played sports or ran. I would go to the gym a little bit, but I was never a PT stud or anything. My close friends and family thought I was going to get drummed out very early on lol.

STREET TALES: *What made you choose the Marine Corps over all the other branches?*

ADAM MACALUSO: I just always loved it. I remember a funny story. I don't think I tell many people this. Remember home economics class in school? We had home economics and we had to sew a little pillow. I sewed this little pillow, olive drab, with black lettering saying USMC on it. I was in sixth grade, and I guess I got caught up in the Marine Corps propaganda.

STREET TALES: *Yeah, fair enough.*

ADAM MACALUSO: I grew watching movies like the *Sands of Iwo Jima* and *Full Metal Jacket*. I always loved those types of movies. I always loved the military. I loved camouflage. I wore camouflage growing up. I just wanted to go to the Marine Corps. I wanted to be a grunt, but considering I had a college degree and could go in as an officer, I thought it would be stupid to not use the tools I had at the time.

When joining the Marine Corps, there are several ways to become a commissioned officer via OCS, ROTC, or if you have already graduated from college. You can also go to the Naval Academy or the Marine Corps Enlisted Commissioning Program.

If you get selected to go to college, then your full-time job is to finish college and then you can get commissioned after that.

I still had a semester of college to go when I went through OCS, which was an ass kicker. I'd never really done anything like that in my life. It wasn't as much the mental mindfuck as bootcamp is for the enlisted guys. They just physically run your ass to the ground, then they put you in a lot of leadership billets for a couple of days.

All you're doing is getting yelled at because no matter what you do, you get yelled at. Even if you do it right, you're still going to get yelled at. Then I graduated, I got commissioned. My dad was happy. My mom wasn't very happy about it, but my parents supported me. I got commissioned in early February 2000. The only way you could be a reserve officer in the Marine Corps was to come in and do active-duty time and then go to the reserves.

The Marine Corps changed that like in 07 or 08 and a lot of guys we're not fans of it. It's nothing against the Marines. You learn a lot when your active duty is as an officer. You get a lot of mentorships from higher ups, your platoon sergeants, and enlisted guys. I wasn't offended. Then you go to this thing called the basic school and that's six months.

That's where all officers in the Marine Corps go, even if you're a pilot, lawyer, anything, no matter what you're going to do, every Marine
officer goes to the basic school and it's six months and most people
hate it. I had the time of my life there. Part of the reason I had such
a good time is that I had a really good staff platoon commander who
was a captain at the time. He's actually a one-star general now. I still
keep in touch with him. Just an awesome officer. A Naval Academy
guy, all-around what you would think of as an awesome officer. He
treated everybody fairly, wasn't a jerk, but just a nice guy. A lot of my
buddies were prior enlisted guys and they were all prior grunts. One of
my buddies is a colonel in MARSOC, another buddy was a colonel, a
MEW Commander, and a couple guys that were grunts went over to
be pilots because they didn't want to be ground pounders anymore.

You go in, and you don't have an M.O.S. The only people that have
M.O.S. are lawyers and then there's air and ground contracts. If you're
an air contract, that means you're going to go to flight school. But if
you don't pass it, they send you back to the ground side even though
you want to be a pilot. Instead, you're going to go be a ground supply
officer or something like that.

There were guys who wanted to be pilots but due to some medical
issue they were not cleared to fly fighter jets and would get moved to
intel or something like that. Other people I know got supply and logistics, and those were things nobody wanted. One of the best officers
I ever met was a guy I was in Central America with. He was a logistics
officer. Phenomenal, phenomenal guy.

He could have supplied the Eastern Front in World War II, and they
would have had full ammunition and everything. That's how good
he was.

STREET TALES: *This is important, especially when you're moving soldiers around all over the world.*

ADAM MACALUSO: You go there, and you do these wish lists when you're there. I don't remember how many when I went there but there were 20 something M.O.S. you could pick from. I went to the TBS company with over 250 guys and gals and there were 30 infantry spots. This is pre-9-11. A lot of tough guys were like, "I'm going to go infantry."

I didn't really know what I wanted to do other than I loved the military, but I didn't know much. At first, I had artillery, and I wanted to do artillery with my good buddy. Then he transitioned, became a grunt and reconnaissance guy. He became an officer and he told me he loved artillery.

If I got artillery leaving TBS, I would be happy. But I also really liked the grunt stuff. I really liked being in the woods, moving, and just being miserable because I was actually pretty decent at it. I was never the fastest runner in this going through training. I was slow as shit. I hate to say it. I put my gear on and I moved, but I was in pain. You just suck it up and you just move, man.

STREET TALES: *People have these dreams of doing certain things, but this shit's hard on your body. Sometimes you just don't have the genetic makeup to do it through no fault of your own. I always thought I wanted to be a pilot, until I realized they're not going to custom fit a fighter jet for this big ass. Not that I ever joined the military, but you start realizing certain things are just not in the cards for you. I was indoctrinated in Marine Corps ideology at a young age as both of my parents are Marines. If you're in the Marine Corps and you wear a Marine uniform, you are a fucking rifleman.*

ADAM MACALUSO: I have a good story about that. We'll get to that in a second. I was at TBS and they had this thing called O and D. We often see defense week and you would be getting hazed by captains and it was miserable. It was raining and everything. But it was like we were doing war games.

I loved the war games, shooting blanks, using the radios, and I was getting paid to do shit I used to with my friends in the backyard! It was awesome. After coming back, we had to put our MOS on a list which was an index card at the time, that's dating me a little. I remember telling the captain at the time, Captain Pretty, I'm changing my MOS list. I had artillery first originally. I gave him a card like from one to 25 that just said infantry, the whole thing. He said, "Okay, I get it."

There were people who were pissed that people who were far better PT years than me. There's envy and normal human emotions. I was excited, all my buddies, Bill, Matt, all these guys got grunts, from my platoon at TBS, 10 of us got infantry, which was pretty impressive.

Then after that, you have to go to infantry officers' course, which was I think, eight weeks, maybe 10 weeks. It's a straight up ass kicker. They straight up fucking hazed us. You shoot, you fight, you're literally ground fighting, boxing.

STREET TALES: *You went from partying in college, jumping around, and now you're a lieutenant in the Marine Corps infantry. Your job is to lead men potentially into war. You actually ended up doing that.*

ADAM MACALUSO: I'm going to jump ahead really quick to when I was with the State Department, Diplomatic Security. I was in Iraq in 2008; second time I was in Iraq with the State Department and I was there on the day they sent agents after that Blackwater incident in 2007. They put the agents one with each Blackwater team.

Aside from my experience with Blackwater, it was all mostly positive. I worked with some absolute professionals. Even guys that did a four-year hitch were like regular infantrymen in the Army and Marine Corps, absolute professionals. That's my experience with it. I have to say that. There are yahoos everywhere. I always like putting that out because a lot of guys I worked with were shit hot. I was supervising this TST, the tactical support team.

Blackwater had the contract for State Department and they would do all the high threat protection, like taking USA State Department employees, all government employees out in Baghdad helping work on the government. I did things like FAA people and undersecretary people through USAID, and stuff like that. But the TST teams would go out and post somewhere in Baghdad in case something like a motorcade got attacked. They would go try and bail it out. We were in Bearcats and we had, two 40s and maybe Mark 19s. We had a lot of weaponry. We had a 12- or 15-man team and I remember going to assist with this other team and there was this guy, a retired army Sergeant first class, which is equal is an E7, equal to a gunnery Sergeant.

I used to have to help with butter bars in the army, and this guy was always bad and busting balls about everything. That's the army. I know, because the army doesn't have the basic school. They don't do like the Marine Corps does. There was this guy, he was a former scout sniper in the Marine Corps and his nickname was Johnny Ringo.

I don't know how he got Johnny Ringo, but he was a nice guy, quiet guy, was what you would think a sniper is, bro. Just cool, calm, collective. I forgot the guy's name that was busting my balls. He told Johnny Ringo that you always had to take care of officers and lieutenants. I told Johnny Ringo I never had that problem in the Marine Corps. All the officers I ever had knew what they were doing.

Johnny told the guy, "Maybe that's the army, but not the Marine Corps and that shut the dude up. I remember that, and that made me so happy.

You go through infantry officers' course and you know a shit ton tactically, but you know nothing administratively in the Marine Corps and, and you know with your background that paperwork makes the dream work. You don't know anything, but part of it is I also learned how to be a Marine from a lot of my enlisted buddies.

From guys that were officers, but they were prior enlisted, I learned how to be a Marine. I learned just to treat them like Marines, and treat them like nice people, treat them how I wanted to be treated. I think that made me money. I got along with my first battalion. I was treating guys like I didn't have anything to prove.

I went through infantry officers' course. I had my rib broken boxing, and then we did ground fighting and a guy threw me and I had all my gear on and landed on my canteen. I sucked it up, but it hurt like hell, man. There were times I wanted to just cry, but I was not redoing that course and I always like to tell this story.

When you get the Infantry Office, of course, there's the common endurance test. There's an indoctrination course. You have to take this test the first day. It's a physical test. When I went, pre-9-11 before the height of Iraq, they said if you fail it, you come in every Saturday till you pass it. I was not failing this thing. First, you have the ground fight. You have to land nav. You have to like run in your gear the whole time, double O courses, more than once. At the end of the day, we went to the classroom and they had all started listing names and they said my name, Macaluso with a few others.

Then they said, "Everybody that we just listed, you guys passed it. Everybody else, next Saturday, you got to come here." There were dudes there who were PT studs, man, and they didn't pass it. I was like, *damn*. That should prove that if just have heart and you just put into it, you can do.

STREET TALES: *I've talked about this on some other episodes. I'm not prior military or anything like that, but law enforcement wise, the biggest stress for me was always the PT tests. You have to pass these things and it's graded on standards. Somebody else was watching you and judging your reps. I enjoy working out, and I've worked for several where I was never a PT stud but passed at least. But then we would do group fitness workouts and several instructors would say, "I don't understand, you crush it in the gym, your energy is great, you're fucking happy, your hype. We love that energy. Then we get to test day and your energy drops?" I just never enjoyed that aspect of training for any of the agencies I ever worked for.*

I'm not knocking people who like to run or want to run or are great at running. I'm just saying that you need both sides. You need some guys who would to be able to go catch the guy and then you need that guy that could rip an arm off.

ADAM MACALUSO: I remember when I got out to the fleet, I had this company commander and he was a machine. I watched him do 37 dead hang pull ups. Perfect. The last two were the only ones he shaked on. A 300 is a perfect PFT. Always a 300. I was his executive officer. He never gave me shit that I couldn't. But he knew I would go out at lunch to swim. When we hiked, he knew I could hang. But it was always hard to get a read on him. But I remember he promoted this kid to corporal who wasn't the embodiment of fitness He didn't even look like what you would think of as a Marine, but he was a good kid. Yeah. I asked the commander why he promoted the kid.

I said, "I always thought you wanted guys that are high first class PFTs." He told me, "You know why I promoted him? Because I've come in on a couple Saturdays to do paperwork and I've seen him running the ridge, knocking pull ups. That's all I want. I just want someone to put the effort in." You know, that's it. That's a big thing in the Marine Corps. There are guys that think you suck because you can't run a sub-18, but there are also guys who are like, all right, man, you didn't quit. You crawled across the finish line, but you did it.

Yeah, you puked after you got through it, but you fucking finished it.

STREET TALES: *I definitely want to get into wartime college kid floating around gets in the military. You're leading men and then boom, wartime happened. Now, shit is real. You're not just a practice hero. Now you're fucking doing it for real.*

ADAM MACALUSO: I was in Okinawa when 9-11 hit. We were deployed and we we're going to fucking war. We knew we're going to Afghanistan. It was in the tea leaves, man, you're going to Iraq. We trained like it was going out of style. That summer we blasted through like two or three years of our battalion's ammo allocation in like a month and a half.

We we're getting closer. It was December and we knew we we're going somewhere. The packing lists came out and we were told to get our stuff packed. I remember sitting there and being told we we're, leaving that night. We were going to March Air Force base and to fly out. I'm like, *holy shit, man, this is fucking real.* We'd been doing all these briefs about the Iraqi army capabilities and all this training to recognize their stuff. We got on the plane and flew to Kuwait at the end of January. We knew that diplomacy was not going to work and the administration wanted to roll in.

STREET TALES: *I am envisioning the movies where you all load up in a C-17 or something, and the music is playing and you're getting ready for war. Is that how it was when you finally deployed?*

ADAM MACALUSO: *No, actually, I flew to war on a Delta flight.* I haven't really flown on a lot of the C-17s in my career. Most guys fly commercial; you're in uniform, and you have layovers and shit.

STREET TALES: *That is blowing my mind, man. You flew to war on a Delta Flight lol!*

ADAM MACALUSO: We were getting ready and I had 57 guys, including myself, when we crossed the border and it was nerve wracking. And to add to it, there was a big chemical threat. We were in mop suits, which is like chemical suits. We had these giant radios with the encryption and everything, I just remember they were really heavy.

I was nervous. I'm not going to lie. We were like contact front or something like that. But that's where your training kicks in and that was always my paranoid thing, getting into combat. We rolled across the border, and I saw the black smoke and I thought, *This is like those videos from the first Gulf War.* Then there were a bunch of T's-55 burning on the side of the road. I remember that there was one I wish I had taken a picture of, but I didn't.

Literally, we cross across the border in Abrams tanks, and I see that one of tanks had hit a mine or something and its track was fucked up. They were fixing it. But these ladies were carrying this Iraqi kid and they tripped and his insides just spilled out, he was dead. It hit me, this is real, dude. This is real. We made a right to where we're going and we're in Amtrak's. We were passing it and on the left is this T-55 tank, and it was burning and there was this black smoke. Soviet tanks they burned and they were flame hazards. I remember this tank burning in the T.C. of the Turk commander, his hatch. There was a fucking skeleton sitting there. Well, he must have been fucking killed instantly because he still looked the way you see in the movies.

Maybe it's been deluded in my mind but from what I remember it was the blackest smoke and that skeleton was as white as could be. We went to our first mission. I don't remember exactly the first time actually pulling the trigger, but I remember I was in the TC and we're getting engaged by Iraqi army regulars, not the Republican guards or something. My hands were shaking, and I was thinking *fuck, I'm scared. In every arena is everybody scared?* If someone says they're not scared, they're lying. I talked to Delta guys and they said, "Yeah, everybody's nervous. You just you keep it in check, man. That's how that's how you do it."

My hand was shaking, and I was afraid I wouldn't be able to engage these guys from the Amtrak. I slapped my hand on the metal of my gun and thought, *okay, I've got this.* I went back and started engaging targets. That's when the training kicks in, everything kicks in. That's what combat is like.

I got buddies that saw a shit ton more combat than I ever did, literally up close and personal in Iraq and Afghanistan. I saw combat, I was in it, but nothing to compare to a lot of my buddies and it's funny because I still feel guilty to this day that I didn't see as much as they did.

When I was out and I was a cop, that's when I volunteered to go to Afghanistan. One of my buddies said, "You did your time." But I explained to him, I feel guilty, bro. Other guys are going. I should go. I'm still able. I'm still a Marine. I want to do it.

I make no illusions. I went to the VA; I talked to the psychiatrist and I remember one of the things I always talked about was how I feel guilty that I wish I had engaged more targets and was in more combat. I never got shot or got killed. I didn't lose any guys under my command. That's a big thing, but I know buddies that lost guys.

Everybody knows when you join the Marine Corps you want to go fight. You want to fucking go kill bad guys. That's what guys want to do. But losing guys is tough. I got cross-decked over to go with another lieutenant because we had too many lieutenants. I went to the battalion commander to say this is bullshit. He said, "Mac, I tried to fight it. You're not a shit bag. We know that, you know?" My battalion commander walked me down to that battalion before we go into Iraq. I still keep in touch with him to this day.

STREET TALES: *Your career is impressive. You had already done your time, but you were on reserve status and you were at hop, but let's backtrack a little bit. After the Marine Corps, was it department of state, how did that flow?*

ADAM MACALUSO: I always wanted to be a cop growing up as well. But I always wanted to have military experience and then go be a cop. I started applying to all the federal agencies. I was living in Arlington at the time. I was still on active duty and I got sent to the Pentagon. That's part of the reason I left active duty.

I always wanted to go to the Diplomatic Security (DS). Always thought DS sounded so fricking cool. I was happy that I got it. I got in the first shot I went through the whole federal hiring process. It's a crap shoot. Some people get it the first shot. Some people have to take like three, four times, but they get it. You know, it's whatever the way the fricking wind is blowing that day.

I was excited. I timed it perfectly. I got to the Department of State. I was coming off active duty. I was on terminal leave, and I went to FLETC and then to do the basic special agent training. I wanted to stay in DC because I had met my now wife at the time, and she was a teacher down there. But the guy who did assignments was from the town next to me up in Jersey. He said, "I hooked you up." I told him, "Your kind of didn't hook me up." He kind of fucked me.

I got sent to the New York field office, which is in Fort Lee, New Jersey. It was a lot of protection, but with DS what was cool is that they're truly a global law enforcement agency because there's RSOs and the regional security officers in every embassy.

You could do these temporary assignments (TDYs) to like Iraq and Afghanistan and places like that. At the time, our sack at the office was only letting guys go to high-threat training that were former military or cops because he was a former Marine in the early eighties. I put in and I got it. The state department, at the time, had this awesome high-threat training program. It's like drinking from a fire hose. If you were in the military, you were okay. But if you never did law enforcement or anything, it's like, *Holy shit.*

They had two former Delta guys running the training. They had a former Green Beret, an 18 Delta who was a medic who was also an SIR instructor. When you think of professionalism, these guys wrote the book on it and they were the nicest dudes to boot. They just wanted to help and wanted to train you. A lot of the firearms guys are former Marines, former snipers, and they train you up really good.

STREET TALES: *That's what you want, especially if you're going into a high threat area. Let me jump in really quick. A lot of people don't know what the department of state does because they only hear about it on the news or in politics when Rubio's going around trying* *to make deals or during wartime. They don't understand what the department of state encompasses. What all do they do and I would like to know more about what you did during your time there.*

ADAM MACALUSO: Diplomatic security, the criminal aspect of the investigation stateside, is passport and visa fraud and then protection of foreign dignitaries below the head of state. Secret Service gets all the presidents and heads of state. We would get like foreign ministers and the like. We did a lot of that. A lot of its smoke and mirrors, and I would think, *why are we guarding this person?*

We would guard someone like The Minister of Corn. I told you about the story about the one lady who was a prosecutor in Italy and the mafia had death threats on her. She did war crimes in Serbia and they give her two agents. I'm like, come on, bro. They do the security for the embassies overseas and they do liaisons with the host nation police and they work with the FBI and DEA when they have people in those offices.

They do a lot with like getting criminals extradition and a lot of protection overseas especially in Iraq and Afghanistan. I was working there in 2007/2008 when they needed people to work in Pakistan. I volunteered to go do it. I was a Marine. I would freaking slide through downtown Baghdad, which when I look back, I think, holy shit, man. I didn't have any flame-resistant stuff on. We would be in armored vehicles, but the D.O.D. wouldn't even let their people go in state vehicles because it wasn't up to standard. An IED would have just vaporized anything.

STREET TALES: *Yeah, people don't think about that.*

ADAM MACALUSO: But we did high-threat protection over in Baghdad, in Iraq. I had an undersecretary for Near Eastern Affairs. I took him up to Mosul. We were in Huey's and took him to Psara. I guarded him. I was the agent in charge for that. We had a Blackwater team. That Blackwater team was shit hot. The shift leader, the second in command, was a 22-year veteran of the navy seals and his clothes were immaculately pressed every day. He was legit. The other guy was like a former green beret who had the beard and everything you've come to expect from a badass navy seal. There was also a Marine Corp Scout Sniper that was also shit hot and had the Marine Corp tats, but again everyone was professional and knew their job.

I loved doing high-threat protection. I had a SIG and an M4. People would think we were Blackwater or something like that. I was a special agent with the United States government, man.

The reason I left DS was my wife. She got a job teaching at the time. It was tough getting a job in Jersey teaching. I felt guilty. *Is this fair that I'm going to drag my wife all over the world?* She'd already been teaching like six or seven years at that time. She had a Master's degree. I had to think about what was best for her. I decided to get out of the U.S. State Department and become a local cop.

STREET TALES: *Before we get on the cop's tension, you told me a story about either Iraq or Iran, but you were in an embassy or something and there was a minister or an official and all the guards were being real squirrely. What was that story? I love that story.*

ADAM MACALUSO: That was the Ministry of Foreign Affairs in Baghdad. At the time, he was a Kurd foreign minister. I had guarded him a bunch in New York City. He was like a very nice guy. He fought Saddam in the eighties during the Iran-Iraq war. He was up in Northern Iraq fighting against Saddam's army. Big dude, he was a warrior back then, he still looked like a warrior.

I guarded the undersecretary for Near Eastern Affairs, Lawrence Butler. Amazing guy. These Iraqi security guys came out in their European type suits, and they all had AKs with their airborne folding stocks on them. And they were mean mugging us, not talking to us. I was right by the Ambassador's Butler and of sudden more security guys came in and the foreign minister came out. He was walking by, he looked at me, and his face lit up. He came over and gave me this big bear hug.

All those Iraqis trying to act all tough, they all had this astonished look. They were like, "How do you know him?" I guarded him in New York City a number of times and, after that, we were like the princes there. They brought us food and tea and it was great. It was the funniest thing because one minute, they we ready to behead us and we're going to be on a video on a gore.com. The next minute, we were hanging out and it was a party. They started showing me pictures of their daughter and half joking about trying to marry her off to one of us.

STREET TALES: *Let's touch on that too. You worked alongside foreign military groups and foreign law enforcement and it's not like our law enforcement, or at least it's not always like that.*

ADAM MACALUSO: I worked with whatever the Iraqi police were at the time after the invasion, often Iran-Iraq war veterans. That was a pretty brutal war, but they had different banks and they were lined up male, female. There were seven or eight lines, and I told Gus, our translator, the Iraqi guy, don't make announcements. Gus was going to do them so we could keep things going well. Then he made an announcement and everybody charged.

It started to stampede, and we had to close it down. I said to Gus, "How would this have been taken care of during Saddam's day?" He said that there may have been one or two cops down there and the first time somebody got out of line, they would have just shot somebody in the head and that would have calmed everything down and put people back in line.

People bitch and moan about the police in the United States, but they would never go out and start shooting people in the head to calm the crowd down. This is how the Iraqi police behave. I watched them beat people in front of us to get them in line. I'm like, my God. Then the Afghan police forget about it. I mean, they were just complete fucking buffoons.

They were high all the time, on either pot or probably opium or something like that. I was in combat with the Brits, and the Brits are shit hot. They know how to fight. People badmouth them, but our special forces, like Deltas, are based off the British S.A.S.

They can fight, man, and they are a professional army. I was in Afghanistan with a lot of other NATO countries. Most of those militaries are a little more laid back than us. But, you know, they're good. The Brits, the Danish, I remember I was hanging out with some Australian S.A.S. guys that were fucking amazing.

The Australian military, I mean, those are professional militaries. I did stuff with the Koreans, the ROK Marine Corps, and the hardest people I've ever met. Would I want to go into combat with them? I'm not really sure.

STREET TALES: *Fair enough.*

ADAM MACALUSO: I want them on our side. They beat their people like it's going out of style; they are big with their discipline and grooming standards. Their maneuvers and strategy, I wasn't too impressed with it, really. I'm biased because I was a Marine. Our guys were better. If you ever get a chance to learn about the rock Marine Corps in Vietnam and during the Vietnam War, it was well known that if they took rounds from the village they would just go and kill everybody in the village.

STREET TALES: *When you and I were talking, it brings memories to mind of the Secret Service. I would work with foreign militaries, foreign law enforcement for visits and overseas or in the United States. I started to get a feel for the different expectations. What I mean by that, like Israel and United Kingdom, most of their, not necessarily local law enforcement, but their version of the Secret Service, all of those guys served in the military in one capacity or another.*

I believe, and I could be wrong and I could be fact-checked, but in Israel, you have to have actually seen combat, which for them probably is easier than some other countries because they're always fighting in order to guard the leader. In the United Kingdom, it's the same thing. They're usually commander or commandos, and they're in MI5 and they're the ones that are doing protection.

Then you go to like Vietnam or Africa or South America, and basically, their secret service and a lot of their police changes with each regime change because the leaders are so concerned that if they get elected and it's the old leaders, guards, or law enforcement, they'll just be overthrown or mutinied. They usually fire them all and, in some cases, execute them. It's amazing to see what they deem as a show of force.

I'll give two examples, and we'll move on. But in Vietnam, I was there with Trump during the APAC. I had a great time and it was very interesting. I've talked about the experience a few times, but basically anywhere you went, the streets were lined with it. It's hard to explain because they all looked like military, but this was their law enforcement. Every mile or so there was some 18 or 19-year-old kid. I'm just going to say that because I don't want to think that they were 14, but they looked very young to me with an AK and they were just standing every mile for 30 or 40 miles. Then you would see them, their military version, which were usually in some sort of black garb, and they were riding around, and they would check on them. The way that they would do things was very different than how you would see in the U.S. Some of the guys and I were out doing some shopping and a black uniform and a peach uniform stopped a kid on a scooter who had a girl on the back.

They said something and yelled at him to get off the scooter. The cop got on the scooter and then they all drove away. I'm like, "Did they just jack that guy's scooter? Like what the fuck is going on?" The kid just kind of threw his hands up, and they started walking somewhere else. Yeah, it's different.

Then you fast forward to when Harris did her swing through Ghana, Zambia, and Tanzania. I think we were in Ghana and there was a similar setup. We had a 20-mile motorcade and every mile or so there was somebody in a black shirt, black BDU pants that said police on it. That's all it said. I asked the driver, "Is this all your police?" He looked at me, and I felt like he didn't want to tell me. He said, "They put out an advertisement two weeks ago that paid all these people $20 to stand there with those shirts on and active law to say, look how big our law enforcement is. They're not cops."

Well, on the pay disparity too, because I know a lot of people, and I'm one of them, bitched about law enforcement pay for a very long *time, but you know, I was talking to the drivers in Africa. They were getting $2, two us dollars, a day to work 12-hour days. I was in Honduras and Pence was down there with Secret Service. That's where I learned about how they switched with every regime change.*

We were using a translator app. He was trying to ask me how much money I made. And I asked him how much money he made. He was very proud that he made $700 a month. This is, very high for that country. I said, "Oh yeah, it's same." Wow, 700 a month and for that those dudes are like putting themselves on the line every day.

ADAM MACALUSO: I did six months in Central America. I was an officer in charge of a security training team. We had teams out there training the military, like Honduras, El Salvador, Guatemala, Belizean, we went to Costa Rica. They don't have a military. They have a national police force, but in El Salvador and the El Salvador Marines, these guys are literally hooking and jabbing every day.

STREET TALES: *I'm still going to bitch about law enforcement pay, absolutely. But you remind me of something else. While we were in Honduras, we got there a day early and we had our day of downtime. Usually when you land with the Secret Service, you go out and explore. A lot of people like to go to the embassy to see stuff or go get food whatever to try to experience wherever you're at. We all went out, and I immediately felt like this isn't safe. There weren't really any local restaurants or shops or anything. It was Wendy's, Walmart, McDonald's, very corporate America stuff that was there in every single place. Like at Chili's, they all had some sort of version of armed guard with a shotgun or an AK-47 guarding each place. I thought, this doesn't feel good. We made it to the embassy and when we got there, the guard's booth had a couple of bullet holes in it.*

"What are you guys doing here? You should not be here." He said, "Get inside. Come on. Come on. on. Come on get inside." He was trying to explain to us that this is not safe. Fast forward to the next day. We were doing our briefing in the RSL when the security officer tells us we should not have left the compound at night. A local citizen got shot in the Chili's.

Some people had gone to just get some food. He's like, "Your life is worth 50 bucks. That cell phone that you have in your pocket is worth half of your salary. They will kill you and rob you just for that cell phone. No questions asked." We said, "Jesus, you should have told us when we got on the fucking plane, bro." We had no idea.

When I try to tell people there is a wealth gap in the United States, but you go to other countries and people that are broke here can still go to Starbucks and get a coffee. People that are broke down there are looking for money to get food.

Here, people are bitching about money and they're talking on their iPhone while they're drinking their Starbucks and complaining that they don't have enough, and I'm like, dude, you have no fucking clue.

Did you know you wanted to get into law enforcement after leaving the military?

ADAM MACALUSO: I did not know initially what I wanted to do after leaving the military and it is a huge change. You come out of the military, high-speed operator, or flying 45-million-dollar jets, and then you have to settle in as a civilian. You get a job, even as a cop, and no one gives a shit about what your experience actually was in the military. Everyone gets lumped into "the military" and what you actually did is forgotten.

I did some pretty cool shit as a federal agent. I stood next to President Bush, Condoleezza Rice, Vice President Cheney, and other world leaders with a loaded gun. You compare that with leading America's youth in combat with a top-secret security clearance, and it's hard to compare the two.

Even with leadership experience and being responsible for millions of dollars in military equipment, I was treated like an inexperienced teenager. It's a hard pill to swallow, but hey, that's the military for you.

STREET TALES: *Switching gears a little, let's talk about firearms training in law enforcement compared to the military. In the Marines, we have established every Marine is a rifleman. I will say that it blows my mind that law enforcement agencies have this aversion to having too many people trained as firearms instructors, like that would be a bad thing?*

ADAM MACALUSO: It's the keeper of the badge or whatever, thinking, *when I went through this course, it was so fucking hard. Now I'm not going to let you go through it.*

My buddy, Matt Danner, asked, "Why are we failing people in Marine Corps schools? We should be making sure people pass as much as possible." I can understand if there's a physical standard or maybe a shooting standard.

STREET TALES: *You brought something up that I actually haven't thought about, but you made a fucking great point. Why do law enforcement agencies and military specialties take pride in failing people. They're almost happy that like only 20 people passed and especially right now, there are so few people who even want to do the job.*

Story Recap

Adam has a vast scope of experience and this conversation only scratches the surface of what Lt. Col. Macaluso has done and been exposed to. This was merely an introduction to Adam and I look forward to digging into his stories and gleaning from his training and unique perspective.

ACKNOWLEDGEMENTS

I would like to express my deepest gratitude to Monte Duncan, David Tarbox, and Joe Caputo for being vulnerable in sharing their stories and their continued friendship throughout this endeavor. I have to give special recognition to the Street Tales team, Bjar Atkins, Monique Greco, and Adam Macaluso. They have given up time with their families, money, and have provided creative support from the very beginning. We are a family and none of this would be possible or as fun without them! I am proud and humble to call all of these amazing individuals my friends and work and build this business with them.

ABOUT THE AUTHOR

Tyler Martin

Tyler Martin, has over 15+ years in law enforcement beginning with the Hillsborough County Sheriff's Office, Maine State Police, and the United States Secret Service. He has served in a variety of different roles throughout his law enforcement career and worked with law enforcement agencies all over the world. Tyler is dedicated to humanizing the badge and sharing the stories of the men and women in law enforcement and those impacted by the profession.

www.ingramcontent.com/pod-product-compliance
Lightning Source LLC
Chambersburg PA
CBHW062136020426
42335CB00013B/1230